A FRAMEWORK: UNDERSTANDING AND WORKING WITH STUDENTS AND ADULTS FROM POVERTY

Payne, Ruby K.
   A framework: understanding and working with students and adults from poverty. Revised edition. Ruby K. Payne ©1995 ii, 240p., Illustrated by Cheryl A. Evans.
   Bibliography p.235-240
   ISBN 0-9647437-3-6

1. Education   2. Sociology   3. Title

RUBY K. PAYNE, PH. D.

CHERYL A. EVANS,
ILLUSTRATOR

A FRAMEWORK: UNDERSTANDING AND WORKING WITH STUDENTS AND ADULTS FROM POVERTY

RFT PUBLISHING

 TABLE OF CONTENTS

A VERY SPECIAL THANKS TO......

...... Judy Duncan, the Assistant Principal at Bowie Elementary who first approached me with the idea.

...... The teachers at Bowie Elementary who were so gracious and receptive of the ideas presented to them.

...... Sara Hector, Field Service agent for Texas Education Agency, whose constant and continuing encouragement and support led to the development of this book.

...... Jay Stailey, Principal at Carver Elementary and President of the National Storytelling Association, whose conversations about poverty and stories stimulated my thinking.

i

...... Karen Coffey, colleague and Project Read consultant, who edited the script and provided suggestions.

...... Carol Ellis, my secretary, who knew the hours I was putting in at home on the book and was supportive.

...... Sue Franta, for all her assistance and support.

...... Cheryl Evans, for her illustrations, editing and layout design.

...... The TEAM project members at the University of Houston-Clear Lake for their interest and encouragement.

ALL MY LOVE TO....

...... Frank and Tom Payne, my husband and son, whose patience, support, encouragement and love have allowed this book to occur.

✔ INTRODUCTION

This book came to be because so many people were asking questions this last year, that finally, I promised to write it down. My name is Ruby Payne and I never realized that the information I had gathered over the years about poverty, middle class, and wealth would be of interest to other people.

It wasn't until an assistant principal, Judy Duncan, came to me and asked about a staff development program for her faculty on discipline and referenced the number of student referrals they were having that I even began talking about the differences. She talked about how the population in the school had changed over the last three years from 24% low income (as measured by the number of students on free and reduced lunch) to 60% low income. As she talked about the kinds of discipline situations they were experiencing, I would explain why those behaviors were happening. Finally, she stopped me and inquired where I was getting my information. It was at that point that I realized that I had been gathering data for 24 years.

Where had I gotten the data? First of all, I have been married for 22 years to my husband, who grew up in poverty because his father died when he was six. Though it was situational poverty, he lived for several years with those who were in generational poverty. Over the years, as I met his family and the many other players in the "neighborhood," I came to realize there were major differences between generational poverty and middle class and that the major differences were not about money. But what put the whole carving into bas relief was the six years we spent in Illinois among the wealthy. It was the adding of the third dimension, wealth, that clarified the differences

3

between and among poverty, middle class, and wealth.

As the principal of an affluent elementary school in Illinois, I began to rethink so much of what I had thought about poverty and wealth. The students had no more native intelligence than the poor students I had worked with earlier in my career. And I noticed that among affluent black, Hispanic, and Asian children, their achievement levels were no different than the white children who were affluent.

So, at Judy Duncan's request, I shared the information with her faculty. They were very interested and thought the information was helpful. One faculty member told another and soon I was doing several workshops in other districts. Sara Hector, a field service agent with Texas Education Agency attended a workshop and told many people about it. Then Jay Stailey, another principal, asked me to come with him to University of Houston-Clear Lake to meet with a grant consortium of which he was a co-chair. This meeting led to more meetings and conversations.

So this information has spread more quickly than I could have ever anticipated. I just hope that this information will be helpful to you, the reader, as well.

SOME KEY POINTS TO REMEMBER

1. **Poverty is relative.** If everyone around you has similar circumstances, the notion of poverty and wealth is vague. Poverty or wealth only exists in relationship to the known quantities or expectation.

2. **Poverty occurs in all races and in all countries.** The notion of a middle class as a large segment of society is a phenomena of this century. The percentage of the population that is poor is subject to definition and circumstance.

6

3. Economic class is a continuous line, not a clear cut distinction. In 1994, poverty line was considered $14,340 for a family of four. In 1994, 7% of the population made more than $100,000. per year. Individuals move and are stationed all along the continuum of income.

4. Generational poverty and situational poverty are different. Generational poverty is defined as being in poverty for two generations or longer. Situational poverty is a shorter time and is caused by circumstance, i.e. death, illness, divorce, etc.

5. **This work is based on patterns. All patterns have exceptions.**

6. **An individual brings with him or her the hidden rules of the class in which s/he was raised.** Even though the income of the individual may rise significantly, many of the patterns of thought, social interaction, cognitive strategies, etc. remain with the individual.

7. **Schools and businesses operate from middle class norms** and use the hidden rules of the middle class. These norms and hidden rules are never directly taught in schools or in businesses.

8. For our students to be successful, we must understand their hidden rules and teach them the rules that will make them successful at school and at work.

9. We can neither excuse them nor scold them for not knowing; as educators we must teach them and provide support, insistence and expectations.

10. To move from poverty to middle class or middle class to wealth, an individual must give up relationships for achievement.

SOME CURRENT STATISTICS ABOUT POVERTY

1. In the United States in 1994, one out of five (21%) individuals under the age of 18 is living in poverty.

2. In 1989, one in three Latino children was living in poverty. Key factors contributing to high Latino child poverty rates include: parents' low hourly earnings, parents' low educational attainment, Latina women's smaller likelihood of working outside the home, and widespread employment discrimination. (Miranda, 1991)

3. Regardless of race or ethnicity, poor children are much more likely than nonpoor children to suffer developmental delay and damage, to drop out of high school, and to give birth during the teen years. (Miranda, 1991)

4. Poverty prone children are more likely to be in single parent families. (Einbinder, 1993) Median female wages in the United States, at all levels of educational attainment, are thirty to fifty percent lower than male wages at the same level of educational attainment. (U.S. Census data, 1993: TSII manual, 1995)

5. Poor inner city youth are seven times more likely to be the victims of child abuse or neglect than are high social-economic-status children. (Renchler, 1993)

6. Poverty is caused by interrelated factors: parental employment status and earnings, family structure, and parental education. (Five Million Children, 1992)

7. In the 1990 census, the following ethnic percentages and numbers of poor children were reported. **

UNITED STATES	NUMBER OF CHILDREN IN POVERTY	PERCENT OF CHILDREN IN POVERTY	PERCENT INCREASE FROM 1980 TO 1990 CENSUS
ALL RACES	11,428,916.	18.3%	14.1%
WHITE	5,876,267.	12.5%	13.1%
AFRICAN-AMERICAN	3,717,128.	39.8%	5.2%
HISPANIC*	2,407,466.	32.2%	10.8%
ASIAN-AMERICAN	346,491.	17.1%	14.5%
NATIVE AMERICAN	260,403.	38.8%	19.2%

* Hispanics may be of any race.

**Chart taken from <u>Making Schools Work for Children in Poverty</u>.

8. While the number of white children in poverty is the largest group, the percentage of minority children in poverty is higher.

✓ CHAPTER ONE: DEFINITIONS AND RESOURCES

To better understand students and adults from

poverty, the definition of poverty will be the "extent

to which an individual does without resources."

These resources will be the following:

15

FINANCIAL - Having the money to purchase goods and services.

EMOTIONAL - Being able to choose and control emotional responses, particularly to negative situations, without engaging in self-destructive behavior. This is an internal resource and shows itself through stamina, perseverance, and choices.

MENTAL - Having the mental abilities and acquired skills (reading, writing, computing) to deal with daily life.

SPIRITUAL - Believing in divine purpose and guidance.

PHYSICAL - Having physical health and mobility.

SUPPORT SYSTEMS - Having friends, family, backup resources available to access in times of need. These are external resources.

ROLE MODELS - Having frequent access to adult(s) who are appropriate, who are **nurturing** to the child, and who do not engage in self-destructive behavior.

KNOWLEDGE OF HIDDEN RULES - Knowing the unspoken cues and habits of a group.

16

Typically, poverty is thought of in terms of financial resources only. However, the reality is that **financial resources**, while extremely important, do not explain the differences in the success with which individuals leave poverty nor the reasons that many stay in poverty. The ability to leave poverty is more dependent upon other resources than it is upon the financial resources. Each of these resources plays a vital role in success of an individual.

Emotional resources provide the stamina to withstand difficult and uncomfortable emotional

17

situations and feelings. Emotional resources are the most important of all resources because, when present, they allow the individual not to return to old habit patterns. In order to move from poverty to middle class or middle class to wealth, an individual must suspend his/her "emotional memory bank" because the situations and hidden rules are so unlike what he/she has experienced previously. Therefore, a certain level of persistence and an ability to stay with the situation until it can be learned and therefore comfortable are necessary. This persistence e.g., staying with the situation is proof that emotional resources are present. Emotional resources come, in part, from role models. **Mental resources** are simply able to process information and use it in daily living. If an individual can read, write, and compute s/he has a decided advantage. The individual can access information from many different free sources as well as be somewhat self-sufficient. **Spiritual resources** are the belief that help can be obtained from a higher power, that there is a purpose for living, and that as an individual, worth and love are given from God. This is a powerful resource because the individual does not see him/herself as hopeless but rather as capable and having worth and value.

Physical resources are having a body that works, that is capable and mobile. The individual can be self sufficient.

A **support system** is a resource. Whom does one go to when help is needed? Those individuals available and who will help are resources. When the child is sick and you have to be at work -- who takes care of the child? Where do you go when money is short and the baby needs medicine? Support systems are not just about meeting financial or emotional needs. They are about knowledge bases as well. How do you get into college? Who helps you when you get rejected? Who helps you negotiate the mountains of paper? Who helps you do your algebra homework when you don't know how to do it? Those people are all support systems.

Role models are resources. All individuals have role models. The question is the extent to which the role model is nurturing or appropriate. Can the role model parent? Work successfully? Provide a gender role for individual? It is from the role model that the individual learns how to live life emotionally.

Knowledge of the hidden rules is crucial to whatever class in which the individual wishes to live. Hidden rules exist in poverty, in middle class and in wealth as well as ethnic groups, etc. Hidden rules are about the salient unspoken understandings that cue the members of the group that this individual does or does not fit. For example, three of the hidden rules in poverty are

21

the following: the noise level is high (the TV is always on, everyone may talk at once), the most important information is non-verbal, and the value of an individual to the group is an ability to entertain.   There are hidden rules about food, dress, decorum, etc.   Generally, to move from one class to the next, it is important to have a spouse or mentor from the class to which you wish to move to model and teach you the hidden rules.

SCENARIOS

These scenarios have been written to portray the cases with which I have been acquainted. These scenarios have deliberately omitted most of the physical, sexual, and emotional abuse that can be present so that the discussion can be about resources.

After each scenario, identify the resources available to the child and those available to the adult.

23

SCENARIO #1:

JOHN AND ADELE

BACKGROUND

John is an eight year old white male. His father is a doctor and remarried but does not see his children. He pays minimal child support. The mother, Adele, works part-time and is an alcoholic. One younger sibling who is mentally and physically handicapped lives with the mother and John.

You are Adele, John's mother. You are a 29 year old white female. You quit college your

24

sophomore year so you could go to work to support John's father as he went through medical school. You were both elated when John was born. During the time your husband was an intern, you found that a drink or two or three in the evening calmed you down, especially since he was gone so much. When your second child was born, she was severely handicapped. Both of you were in shock; a year later your husband finished his residency and announced that he was in love with another woman and divorced you. Last you heard, your husband is driving a Porsche and he and his new wife spent their last vacation in Cancun. Your parents are dead. You have a sister who lives 50 miles away. Your weekly income including child support is $300 before taxes. Your handicapped child is three years old and is in day care provided by the school district.

CURRENT SITUATION

You have been late for the third time this month to work. Your car broke down and it will take $400 to fix it. Your boss told you that you will be docked for a day's pay and that if you are late again, you will be fired. You don't know how you are going to get to work tomorrow. You consider several choices: (1) you can go car shopping, (2) you can put the car in the garage and worry about the money later, (3) you can invite the mechanic over for dinner, (4) you can get mad and quit, (5) you can call your ex and threaten to take him back to court unless he pays for the car, (6) you can get a second job, or (7) you can get drunk.

Your daughter has had another seizure and you took her to the doctor (one of the reasons you were late for work). The new medicine will cost you $45 every month.

John comes home from school and announces that the school is going to have a reading contest. Every book you read with him will earn points for him. Each book is one point and he wants to earn 100 points. You must do physical therapy with your daughter each evening for 30 minutes as well as get dinner. To get his books, he needs you to go to the library with him. You only have enough gas to go to work and back for the rest of the week, maybe not that. He also tells you that the school is having an open house and he will get a pencil if you come. But John is not old enough to keep your daughter. Your ex has already threatened to bring up in court that you are an unfit mother if you try to get more money from him.

The mechanic calls and invites you out to dinner. He tells you that you might be able to work something out in terms of payment. It has been a long time since you have been out and he is nice and good looking.

What are Adele and John's resources? Put a check under the resources that are present, a minus under the ones that are not, and a question mark where the resources are uncertain.

Financial	
Emotional	
Mental	
Spiritual	
Physical	
Support Systems	
Knowledge of middle class hidden rules	
Role Models	

SCENARIO #2

VANGIE AND OTIS

BACKGROUND

Otis is a nine year old black male. His mother conceived him at 14, dropped out of school and is on welfare. Otis has two younger siblings and one older sibling who is a gang member.

You are Otis's mother, Vangie. You are a twenty-three year old black female. You were the oldest of five children. You had your first child when you were 14. You have received welfare and food stamps since the birth of your first child. You lived with your mother until your fourth child was born when you were 17. Then you got your own place. You dropped out of school when you were pregnant with Otis. School was always difficult for you and you never did feel comfortable reading much anyway. Your current boyfriend comes often and he works sometimes. Your mother lives down the street. Your weekly income (including food stamps) is $215. You move a lot because there are always more bills at the end of the month than money.

CURRENT SITUATION

Your sister calls you and tells you that her boyfriend has beaten her again and she needs to come spend the night at your house. The last time she came she stayed for two weeks and her twelve year old handicapped son would not leave your five year old daughter alone. You have several choices: (1) you could take her in and make her pay for her meals, (2) you could not take her in and have the whole family mad at you, (3) you could tell your daughter to hit him when he comes close, (4) you could make Otis take care of the handicapped son, (5) you could slap the fool out of the handicapped son, (6) you could use the rent money for the extra food, (7) you could go partying together and let Otis take care of the kids; (8) you could move to a bigger place.

Otis comes home from school and announces that the school is going to have a reading contest. For every five books you read to him, he will get a coupon to get $2.00 off a pizza. To get his books, he needs you to go to the library. Also you are not sure you can even read to him because your skills were never good and you have not read for a long time. To get to the library requires that you walk because you do not have a car. There have been two drive by shootings last week. He also tells you that the school is having an open house and is sending a bus around the neighborhood to pick up parents. He gives you a note which you cannot read.

You are going to have to move again. This week Otis got cut badly at school and the school took him to the emergency room and they want $200. Rent is due for the month and it is $300 for three bedrooms. Sister is coming and that means extra food because she never has any money. Your boyfriend got arrested and wants you to get him out of jail. He was arrested for assault. The bondsman wants $500. Your ex-boyfriend knew better than to come around. You need your boyfriend because his money makes it possible to keep from going hungry.

The teacher calls and tells you that Otis is misbehaving again. You beat the fool out of him with a belt and tell him he better behave. But that night you fix him his favorite dinner, then you tell everyone that you talk to how Otis is behaving and what a burden he is to you.

What are Vangie and Otis's resources? Please put a check under the resources that are present, a minus under the ones that are not, and a question mark where the resources are uncertain.

Financial	
Emotional	
Mental	
Spiritual	
Physical	
Support Systems	
Knowledge of middle class hidden rules	
Role Models	

SCENARIO #3:

OPRAH AND OPIE

BACKGROUND

Opie is a 12 year old black female and the oldest of five children. She runs the household because her mother, Oprah, works long hours as a domestic. Grandmother, who is 80, is senile and lives with them, as well as an out of work uncle.

You are Opie's mother, Oprah. You are a 32 year old black female. You were married for ten years to your husband and then he was killed in a car accident on the way to work two years ago. You work long hours as a domestic for a doctor. You go to the Missionary Baptist Church every Sunday where you lead the choir. Your employer treats you well and you take home about $300 every week. You ride public transportation to work and the church bus on Sunday. You want your children to go to college even though you only finished high school.

CURRENT SITUATION

Your employer gives you a $400 Christmas bonus. You thank the Lord at church for the gift. After church, three different people approach you privately. One asks for $50 to pay to have the electricity turned on; one asks for $100 to feed her brother's family; one asks for $60 to replace a pair of broken glasses. You were hoping to save some money for an emergency.

Opie has the opportunity to be in a state-sponsored competition that requires after school presence.. You want her to do that but you must have her at home after school every day.

What resources do Oprah and Opie have? Put a check under the resources that are present, a minus under the ones that are not, and a question mark where the resources are uncertain.

Financial	
Emotional	
Mental	
Spiritual	
Physical	
Support Systems	
Knowledge of middle class hidden rules	
Role Models	

SCENARIO #4:

MARIA AND NOEMI

BACKGROUND

Maria is a ten year old Hispanic female. Her mother does not drive or speak English. Father speaks some English. Maria is a second generation Hispanic born in the United States. Mother does not work. Father works for minimum wage as a concrete worker. There are five children. The family gets food stamps and the mother is a devout Catholic.

35

You are Maria's mother, Noemi. You are a 27 year old Hispanic female. You have five children. You have been married to your husband for 11 years and you love him and your children very much. Children always come first. As a child, you and your parents were migrant workers so you are happy that you have a place to live and do not need to move around. Because of the migrant work, you never went past the sixth grade. Your husband works on a construction crew laying concrete. When it is not raining and when there is plenty of building, he has plenty of work. Sometimes though, he will go two or three weeks with no work and therefore, no money. Your parents live in your town and they help you when times are bad. You get food stamps to help out. You go to Mass every Saturday and often on the weekends you go to your parents with your children and brothers and sisters. Your husband is a good man and he loves his children. On a good week, he will bring home $400.

CURRENT SITUATION

Maria comes home and says that she has to do a salt map. You have just spent all the money for the week on food and she needs five pounds of flour, two pounds of salt and a piece of board to put it on. She also needs to get information from an encyclopedia, whatever that is. The car is broken and will take $100 for parts. The baby is sick and medicine will be $30.00. It has rained for two weeks and your husband has not had any work or pay.

The teacher has asked Maria to stay after school and be in an academic contest. You expect her to get married and have children just as you have. You need her to help you with the children.

What resources do Maria and Noemi have? Put a check under the resources that are present, a minus under the ones that are not, and a question mark where the resources are uncertain.

Financial	
Emotional	
Mental	
Spiritual	
Physical	
Support Systems	
Knowledge of middle class hidden rules	
Role Models	

SCENARIO #5:

EILEEN AND

WISTERIA

BACKGROUND

Eileen is a ten year old white girl who lives with her 70 year old grandmother, Wisteria, who is on social security. She does not know who her father is. Her mother has been arrested four times for prostitution and/or drug possession in the last two years. About once a year, mother sobers up for a month and wants Eileen back as a child.

You are Eileen's grandmother, Wisteria. You are on social security and get about $150 a week. Your daughter, Eileen's mother, has been in trouble for years. You have given up on her and you could not stand to see Eileen in a foster home so you have taken her into your home. Eileen's mother was never sure who the father was; she is a drug addict and has been frequently arrested. One of her various pimps or boyfriends gets her out of jail. Once a year, she sobers up for a short period of time, gives Eileen lots of attention, and then leaves. The last time she came and left, Eileen cried and cried and said she never wanted to see her mother again. You have some money in savings but you do not want to use it. Your house is paid for and you have a decent car. You worry what will happen to Eileen if you would get sick or die, and you pray each day to live until Eileen is 18. You don't see as well as you once did. All your relatives are either dead or distant. Every Sunday, you and Eileen go to the Methodist Church where you have been a member for forty years.

CURRENT SITUATION

Eileen came home from school today with a project to do. She must do a family history and interview as many relatives as possible. You are not sure what to say to Eileen.

The teacher tells you at a conference that Eileen has an imaginary friend that she talks to a great deal during the day and recommends that

39

you seek counseling for Eileen. She knows a counselor who would only cost $40 a session. She also comments that Eileen's clothes are old fashioned and that she does not fit in with the other students. You do not tell the teacher that you make Eileen's clothes. The teacher suggests that you let Eileen have friends over so she can socialize, but you don't know if you can stand the noise.

What are Eileen and Wisteria's resources? Put a check under the resources that are present, a minus under the ones that are not, and a question mark where the resources are uncertain.

Financial	
Emotional	
Mental	
Spiritual	
Physical	
Support Systems	
Knowledge of middle class hidden rules	
Role Models	

SCENARIO #6:

JUAN AND RAMON

BACKGROUND

Juan is a six year old male Hispanic who lives with his uncle Ramon. Juan's father was killed in a gang-related killing. His uncle is angry about the death of Juan's father. When his uncle is not around, Juan stays with his grandmother, who speaks no English. The uncle makes his living selling drugs but is very respectful of his mother.

You are Juan's uncle, Ramon, a 25 year old Hispanic male. You doubt that you will live many

41

more years because you know that most of the people like you are either dead or in jail. You are angry. Your brother, Juan's father, was killed by a rival gang two years ago when Juan was 4. Juan is your godchild and you will defend him with your blood. Juan's mother was a piece of white trash and would not take care of Juan like a good mother should. She is in jail now for gang-related activities. You leave Juan with your mother often because the activities you are involved in are too dangerous for Juan to be with. you. You are a leader in your gang and sell drugs as well. Your mother speaks only Spanish but you have taught Juan to be very respectful to her. She goes to mass every Sunday and takes Juan with her when she can. You make $1000 a week on the average.

CURRENT SITUATION

Juan comes home with a parent-teacher conference request. You are away, hiding from the police. Grandmother cannot read Spanish or English.

The rival gang has killed another one of your gang members. This has forced you to be away from Juan more than you would like. Plans are that you will kill the leader of the rival gang, but then you will need to go to Mexico for some time to hide. You are thinking about taking Juan with you because he is all in the world that you love. You

42

are stockpiling money and you don't want to take him out of school but he is only six. He can catch up. You don't think you will live past 30 and you want to have time with him.

What resources do Juan and Ramon have? Put a check under the resources that are present, a minus under the ones that are not, and a question mark where the resources are uncertain.

Financial	
Emotional	
Mental	
Spiritual	
Physical	
Support Systems	
Knowledge of middle class hidden rules	
Role Models	

SCENARIO #7:

SUEANN AND SALLY

BACKGROUND

Sally is an eight year old white female whose mother, SueAnn, has been married and divorced twice. Her mother works two jobs and does not receive child support. An older sister is pregnant. Sally has two step-siblings, one younger and one older. The current stepfather's favorite child is the youngest child, a son. The stepfather is laid off right now.

You are Sally's mother, SueAnn, a 33 year old white female. You are on your third marriage. You have four children by four different men. You are working two jobs right now because your current husband has been laid off. He is supposed to be

44

taking care of the kids, but he doesn't like to be tied down. You got pregnant when you were a senior in high school, so were unable to finish school. You knew who the father was but he changed his mind and would not marry you. You kept the child and she is now 15 and pregnant. Your second child is Sally and she is 8 years old. Between the two jobs you bring home about $400 a week and you are exhausted. You make the girls cook and clean. You are very tired. Lately you and your husband have been fighting a lot. Your mother and father are divorced and live in the same town that you do. You remember how much you loved to dance country western and party. All you wish for now is sleep. You may have to move again soon because you are so behind on the bills.

CURRENT SITUATION

You get a call at work. You let your husband drop you off at work because he was going to fix the muffler. Your husband is now in jail. He was caught driving while intoxicated. This is the second time he has been caught. You need $500 to pay the bondsman to get him out of jail. Furthermore, he was driving your car which did not have car insurance. They have towed the car and the towing bill is $80. Each day it is impounded, it will cost you $40 in parking fees and you cannot get the car out until you have proof of insurance. When and if he gets out of jail, he will need to see the probation

45

officer, which will cost him $60 every time he sees him.

Your pregnant daughter needs $400 to pay the doctor so he will continue to see her. You have told her she needs to go to the clinic where the service is free. However, the wait is usually 3 to 4 hours and she misses a half day of school. There is also the problem of getting her there. It is in a bad part of town and it will be dark before you can get there to pick her up.

The bill collector calls you at work and tells you he is going to take you to court for overdue electric bills at the last place you lived. You now live in an apartment where the utilities are paid but you are behind on your rent by a month. You were O.K. until your husband got laid off. You are out of birth control pills yourself. To refill the prescription, you have to go to the clinic and wait 3 to 4 hours and you can not take time off from work. Also, you need $20.00 for the birth control pills. Lately your husband has been looking at Sally in ways that you do not like. But you are so tired.

What are SueAnn and Sally's resources? Put a check under the resources that are present, a minus under the ones that are not, and a question mark where the resources are uncertain.

Financial	
Emotional	
Mental	
Spiritual	
Physical	
Support Systems	
Knowledge of middle class hidden rules	
Role Models	

DISCUSSION OF

SCENARIOS

Significantly, each scenario illustrates a variance in the amount and kinds of resources available, as well as a variation on the theme of poverty. In marking the scenarios, this would be the manner in which the resources might be identified.

Resource	#1	#2	#3	#4	#5	#6	#7
Financial	n	n	n	n	?	y	y
Emotional	n	n	y	y	?	n	n
Mental	y	n	y	y	y	y	y
Spiritual	n	n	y	y	y	y	n
Physical	y	y	y	y	y	y	y
Support Systems	n	n	y	y	y	y	n
Knowledge of middle class hidden rules	y	n	y	n	y	n	n
Role Models	?	n	y	y	?	n	n

Knowledge of the hidden rules is marked in relationship to the knowledge base the individual has about middle class rules. Each of the scenarios has aspects which are unique to poverty.

For example, the jail incident in the SueAnn scenario is one. For many individuals who live in poverty, jail is a part of their lives on a fairly frequent basis for several reasons. First of all, if an individual is in generational poverty, organized society is viewed with distrust and distaste. The line between what is legal and illegal is thin and frequently crossed. A lack of resources means that the individual will need to spend periods of time in jail for crossing those lines because he does not have the resources to avoid it. The reality is that middle class and upper class also cross the lines, but not with the frequency of those in poverty. In addition, the upper and middle class have the resources to avoid jail. The poor simply see jail as a part of life and not necessarily always bad. Local jails provide food and shelter and as a general rule are not as violent or dangerous as a state incarceration. SueAnn will most probably get her husband out of jail because relationships are also more important in generational poverty than is money.

Another example of a characteristic of poverty is the incident with Oprah at church, where she receives the extra money and is immediately besieged with requests. One of the hidden rules of poverty is that any extra money is shared. Middle class puts a great deal of emphasis on being self-sufficient. In poverty, the clear understanding is that one will never get ahead so when extra money is available, it is either shared or immediately spent. There are always emergencies and needs; one might as well enjoy the moment. Oprah will share the money; she has no choice. If she does not, the next time she is in need, she will be left in the cold. It is the hidden rule of the support system. In poverty, people are possessions and people can only rely on each other. It is absolutely imperative that the needs of an individual come first. After all, that is all you have - people.

The discipline incident in Vangie and Otis is included because another aspect of generational poverty is that discipline is about penance and forgiveness, not about change. The mother is the most powerful figure in generational poverty. Not only does she control the limited resources, she is also the "keeper of the soul." She gives out penance and forgiveness. The typical pattern in poverty for discipline is to severely verbally chastise the child or physically beat the child, then forgive him/her and feed him. The hidden rules about food in poverty is that food is equated with love. In the final analysis, all you have are people. How do you show people that you love them? You give them food so they can continue to live. One of the mistakes educators make is to misunderstand the role of punishment in generational poverty. Punishment is not about change; individuals in poverty believe in fate and destiny. Punishment is about penance and forgiveness. Therefore, to expect changed behavior after a parent-teacher conference is a false hope.

The Juan/Ramon incident is included to make some points about the role of violence and gangs in poverty. Gangs are a type of support system. They provide virtually all of the resources needed for survival. Fighting and physical violence are a part of poverty. People, living in poverty, need to be able to defend themselves physically or they need someone to be their protector. Middle class uses space to deal with conflict and disagreement, i.e. they go to a different room and cool off; they purchase enough land so they are not encroached upon; they live in neighborhoods where people keep their distance. But in poverty, this is not

54

possible. The only way to defend turf is physically.

Also, individuals in poverty are not going to call the police for two reasons: first, the police may be looking for them; second, the police are going to be slow to respond. Why bother?

The Wisteria/Eileen scenario is included because of the growing number of children living with grandparents and the effect that has on the emotional resources of the children.   Emotional resources come from observing role models deal with adverse situations and social interactions. Eileen will come out of the situation knowing that she does not want to be like her mother, but also that she does not want to be like her grandmother.

So it will be difficult for her to identify an appropriate female role model. To have emotional resources that are healthy, one needs to have an identity. One uses role models to build that identity. Because of the limited financial resources of her grandmother, Eileen's access to appropriate role models will be limited to church and school.

The John/Adele scenario highlights the number of children who are in situational poverty because of divorce. Adele is making the slide from middle class to poverty and she does not know the rules of poverty. Adele is an example of what happens when an individual allows her difficulties to erode her emotional resources. Because of her alcoholism, she is emotionally weak. (The reverse is also true, i.e. her emotional weakness leads to her dependence on alcohol.) Of all the resources, emotional resources seem to be paramount in maintaining a lifestyle with some semblance of order. When emotional resources are absent, the slide to poverty is almost guaranteed. But because her financial resources are limited, she must learn the rules of generational poverty. And one of the rules in generational poverty for women is this: you may need to use your body for survival. After all, that is all that is truly yours. Sex will bring in money and favors. Values are important but they do not put food on the table nor bring relief from intense pressure. So Adele will most probably go out with the mechanic for two reasons: (1) she can get her car fixed and (2) she can have an evening out on the town.

Maria and Noemi are included because they represent the classic Hispanic pattern of poverty. In the Hispanic poverty pattern, the majority of families are two parent. As can be seen, of all the scenarios, they have more resources than any of the others.

In conclusion, the resources an individual has varies tremendously from situation to situation. Poverty is more about other resources than it is about money. The other resources are those that educators can influence tremendously.

WHAT DOES THIS INFORMATION MEAN IN THE SCHOOL OR WORK SETTING?

*   Resources of students and adults should be analyzed before dispensing advice or seeking solutions to the situation. What may seem to be very workable suggestions from a middle class point of view may be virtually impossible given the resources available to those in poverty.

*   Educators have tremendous opportunities to influence some of the non-financial resources that make such a difference in student's lives. It costs nothing to be an appropriate role model, for example.

✔CHAPTER TWO: THE ROLE OF LANGUAGE AND STORY

To better understand poverty, one must understand three aspects of language: registers of language, discourse patterns, and story structure. Many of the key issues for schools and businesses are related to these three patterns that often are different in poverty than they are in middle class .

REGISTERS OF LANGUAGE

Every language in the world has five registers. (Joos, 1967.) These registers are the following:

61

REGISTER	EXPLANATION
FROZEN	Language that is always the same. For example: Lord's Prayer, wedding vows, etc.
FORMAL	The standard sentence syntax and word choice of work and school. Has complete sentences and specific word choice.
CONSULTATIVE	Formal register when used in conversation. Discourse pattern not quite as direct as formal register.
CASUAL	Language between friends and is characterized by a 400-500 word vocabulary. Word choice general and not specific. Conversation dependent upon non-verbal assists. Sentence syntax often incomplete.
INTIMATE	Language between lovers or twins. Language of sexual harassment.

RULE: JOOS FOUND THAT ONE CAN GO ONE REGISTER DOWN IN THE SAME CONVERSATION AND THAT IS SOCIALLY ACCEPTED. HOWEVER, TO DROP TWO REGISTERS OR MORE IN THE SAME CONVERSATION IS TO BE SOCIALLY OFFENSIVE

How then does this register impact students from poverty? First of all, the work of Dr. Maria

Montano-Harmon (Montano-Harmon, 1991) found that the majority (of the students in her research) of minority students and poor students do not have access to formal register at home. As a matter of fact, these students cannot use formal register. The problem is that all the state tests, SAT, ACT, etc. are in formal register. It is further complicated by the fact that to get a well-paying job, it is expected that one will be able to use formal register. Ability to use formal register is a hidden rule of middle class. The inability to use it will knock one out of an interview in two or three minutes. The use of formal register allows one to score well on tests and do well in school and higher education.

This use of formal register is further complicated by the fact that these students do not have the vocabulary or the knowledge of sentence structure and syntax to use formal register. When student conversations in the casual register are observed, much of the meaning comes not from the word choices, but from the non-verbal assists. To be asked to communicate in writing without the non-verbal assists is an overwhelming and formidable task which most of them try to avoid. It has very little meaning for them.

DISCOURSE PATTERNS IN FORMAL AND CASUAL REGISTER

This pattern of registers is connected to the second issue: the patterns of discourse. Discourse will be discussed here with two different meanings. The first meaning will be the manner in which the information is organized. In the formal register of English, the pattern is to get straight to the point. In casual register, the pattern is to go around and around and finally get to the point. For students who have no access to formal register, educators become very frustrated with the tendency of these students to meander seemingly meaninglessly through a topic. It is simply the manner in which information is organized in casual register.

LANGUAGE ACQUISITION IN PRIMARY AND SECONDARY DISCOURSE

The other meaning associated with discourse will be the (Gee, 1987) notion of primary and secondary discourse issues. Primary discourse is the language an individual first acquired. Secondary discourse is the language of the larger society that the individual must be able to use to function in the larger society. For example, if a student has as his/her primary discourse casual register of Spanish, then he/she must also learn formal register of English in order to fully negotiate and participate in the larger society of America. Gee points out that students do much better in school when their primary discourse is the same as the secondary discourse.

RAMIFICATIONS

Gee (1987) then makes a distinction between acquisition and learning. Acquisition is the best and most natural way to learn a language and is simply the immersion and constant interaction in that language. Learning is the direct teaching of a language and usually is at a more metacognitive level. However, what Gee does not talk about is the following: acquisition of language only occurs when there is a significant relationship. That then leads to the next question: To what extent can a formal institution create significant relationships? Just think -- would you learn to use sign language well if there were no significant relationship that called for that usage? Would you learn to speak Chinese well if there were no significant relationship?

Therefore, when we ask students to move from casual to formal register, we almost need to direct teach it. Natural acquisition of formal register would require a significant relationship.

In the work of Montano-Harmon, she found that for students to move from casual register English to formal register English required students to translate because the word choice, sentence syntax, and discourse pattern was different. This translation becomes much more meaningful if there is a significant relationship. However, if there is not a significant relationship, then the instruction must be more direct.

PATTERNS OF DISCOURSE

In the oral language tradition in which the casual register operates, the pattern of discourse is quite different. Discourse is defined as the organizational pattern of the information.

FORMAL REGISTER DISCOURSE PATTERN

SPEAKER OR WRITER GETS STRAIGHT TO THE POINT.

CASUAL REGISTER DISCOURSE PATTERN

WRITER OR SPEAKER GOES AROUND THE ISSUE BEFORE COMING TO THE POINT.

How does this make a difference for students and teachers? First of all, parent-teacher conferences tend to be misunderstood on both sides. Teachers want to get right to the point; parents, particularly those from poverty, want to go around the bush first.

70

When teachers cut the conversation and get right to the point, parents view that as being rude and non-caring. Secondly, writing for students becomes particularly difficult because they wish to go around the bush and not meet the standard organizational pattern of getting to the point in a salient way. This discourse pattern is coupled with the third pattern, that of story structure.

Story Structure

THE FORMAL REGISTER STORY STRUCTURE STARTS AT THE BEGINNING OF THE STORY AND GOES TO THE END IN A CHRONOLOGICAL OR ACCEPTED NARRATIVE PATTERN. THE MOST IMPORTANT PART OF THE STORY IS THE PLOT.

71

THE CASUAL REGISTER STORY STRUCTURE BEGINS WITH THE END OF THE STORY FIRST OR THE PART WITH THE GREATEST EMOTIONAL INTENSITY. THE STORY IS TOLD IN VIGNETTES WITH AUDIENCE PARTICIPATION IN BETWEEN. THE STORY ENDS WITH A COMMENT ABOUT THE CHARACTER AND HIS/HER VALUE. THE MOST IMPORTANT PART OF THE STORY IS THE CHARACTERIZATION.

To understand this story structure better, the story of Cinderella will be told both ways.

FORMAL REGISTER VERSION (abbreviated because of familiarity)

Once upon a time, there was a girl named Cinderella. She was very happy and she lived with her father. Her father remarried a woman who had three daughters. When Cinderella's father died, her step-mother treated Cinderella very badly and, in fact, made her the maid for herself and her three daughters. At the same time in this land, the King decided that it was time for the Prince to get married. So, he sent a summons to all the people in the kingdom to come to a ball. Cinderella was not allowed to go but was forced to prepare her

73

step-sisters and step-mother for the ball. After they left for the ball and as Cinderella was crying on the hearth, her fairy godmother came and with her magic wand, gave Cinderella a beautiful dress, glass slippers, and a stagecoach made from pumpkins and mice; she then sent Cinderella to the ball in style. There was one stipulation: she had to be back home by midnight.

At the ball, the Prince was completely taken by Cinderella and danced with her all evening. As the clock began striking midnight, Cinderella remembered what the fairy godmother had said and fled from the dance. All she left was one of her glass slippers.

The Prince held a big search using the glass slipper as a way to identify the missing woman. He finally found Cinderella, she could wear the glass slipper; he married her and they lived happily ever after.

CASUAL REGISTER VERSION (Audience participation is in normal print. Narrator is in bold print.)

Well, you know Cinderella married the Prince, in spite of that old nasty step-mother. Pointy eyes - that one. Old hag! **Good thing she had a fairy godmother or she would have never made it to the ball.** Lucky thing! God bless her ragged tail! Wish I had me a fairy godmother. **And to think that she nearly messed up big time by staying until the clock was striking twelve. After all the fairy godmother had done for her.** Um Um. She shoulda known better. Eyes too full of the Prince they were. They didn't call him the Prince for no reason. **When she got to the ball, her step-sisters and step-mother didn't even recognize her she was so beautiful without those rags.** Served them right - no good jealous people. **The Prince just couldn't quit dancing with her, just couldn't leave his eyes off her. He had finally found his woman.** Lucky her! Lucky him! Sure wish life was a fairy tale. Kinda like the way I met Charlie. Ha Ha. **The way she arrived was something else - a coach and horseman - really elegant. Too bad when she ran out of there**

as the clock struck 12 that all that was left was a pumpkin rolling off and four mice! What a surprise for the mice! **Well he has to find her because his heart is broken. So he takes the glass slipper and hunts for her and her old wicked step-mother, of course, is hiding her.** What a prize! Aren't they all? **But he finds her and marries her. Somebody as good as Cinderella deserved that.** Sure hope she never invited that step-mother to her castle. Should make her the maid!!

The End

As is readily obvious, the second story structure is far more entertaining, more participatory and exhibits a richness of character, humor, and feeling that is absent from the first version. The first version has sequence, order, cause and effect, and a conclusion; all skills necessary for problem-solving, inference, etc.

Cognitive studies indicate that story structure is a way that the brain stores memories. Given the first story structure, memories would be stored more sequential and thinking patterns would follow story structure. Feuerstein (1980) notes the episodic, nearly random memory and its adverse effects on thinking.

WHAT CAN SCHOOLS DO TO ADDRESS CASUAL REGISTER, DISCOURSE PATTERNS, AND STORY STRUCTURE?

Because there is such a direct link between achievement and language, it must be addressed. The following suggestions are not inclusive, but rather a place to begin.

77

1. Have students write in the casual register and translate to the formal register.

2. Make part of the discipline plan that students learn how to express their displeasure in the formal register and therefore not be reprimanded.

3. Use graphic organizers to show patterns of discourse.

4. In the classroom, tell stories both ways. Tell the story using the formal register story structure then tell the story with the casual register structure. Talk about how the stories change, how they stay the same, and how they are different.

5. Allow for participation in the writing and telling of stories.

6. Use stories in math, social studies, and science to develop concepts.

7. Make up stories with the students which can be used to guide behavior.

WHAT DOES THIS INFORMATION MEAN IN THE SCHOOL OR WORK SETTING?

***   Formal register needs to be directly taught.

***   Casual register needs to be recognized as the   primary discourse for many students.

***   Discourse patterns need to be directly taught.

***   Both story structures need to be used as a part of classroom instruction.

***   Discipline which occurs when a student uses the   inappropriate register should be used as a time for instruction in the appropriate register.

80

***   Students need to be told how much the formal register affects their abilities to get a good paying job.

✔CHAPTER THREE: HIDDEN RULES AMONG CLASSES

Hidden rules are the unspoken cues and habits of a group. Distinct cueing systems exist between and among groups and economic classes. Generally, in America, that notion is recognized for racial and ethnic groups but not particularly for economic groups. There are many hidden rules to examine. The ones examined here are those which have the most impact on

schools and success in the workplace.

But, first......

A LITTLE QUIZ...

COULD YOU SURVIVE IN POVERTY? Put a check beside the items you know how to do.

_____ 1. I know which churches and sections of town have the best rummage sales.

_____ 2. I know which rummage sales have "bag sales" and when.

_____3. I know which grocery stores' garbage bins can be accessed for thrown away food.

_____4. I know how to get someone out of jail.

_____5. I know how to physically fight and can defend myself physically.

_____6. I know how to get a gun even if I have a police record.

_____7. I know how to keep my clothes from being stolen at the laundromat.

_____8. I know what problems to look for in a used car.

_____9. I know how to live without a checking account.

_____10. I know how to live without electricity and without a phone.

_____11. I know how to use a knife as scissors.

_____12. I can entertain a group of friends with my personality and my stories.

_____13. I know what to do when I don't have
money to pay the bills.

_____14. I know how to move in one-half day.

_____15. I know how to feed 8 people for 5 days
on $25.

_____16. I know how to get and use food stamps.

_____17. I know where the free medical clinics
are.

_____18. I am very good at trading and bartering.

_____19. I can live without a car.

COULD YOU SURVIVE IN MIDDLE CLASS?
Put a check beside those items you know how to do.

_____1. I know how to get my children in Little League, piano lessons, soccer, etc.

_____2. I know how to properly set a table.

_____3. I know which stores are most likely to carry the clothing brands my family wears.

_____4. My children know the best name brands in clothing.

_____5. I know how to order in a nice restaurant.

_____6. I know how to use a credit card, checking account, savings account and understand an annuity. I understand term life insurance, disability insurance, 20/80 medical insurance policy as well as house insurance, flood insurance, and replacement insurance.

_____7. I talk to my children about going to college.

_____8. I know how to get one of the best interest rates on my new car loan.

_____9. I understand the difference among the principal, interest, and escrow statements on my house payment.

_____10.I know how to help my children with their homework and do not hesitate to call the school if I need additional information.

_____11.I know how to decorate the house for the different holidays.

_____12.I know how to get a library card.

_____13. I know how to use the different tools in the garage.

_____14. I repair items in my house immediately when they break or know a repair service and call it.

COULD YOU SURVIVE IN WEALTH? Put a check by each item that you know how to do.

_____1. I can read a menu in French, English, and another language.

_____2. I have several favorite restaurants in different countries of the world.

_____3. During the holidays, I know how to hire a decorator to identify the appropriate themes and items with which to decorate the house.

_____4. I know who my preferred financial advisor, legal service, designer, domestic employment service, and hairdresser are.

_____5. I have at least two residences which are staffed and maintained.

_____6. I know how to ensure confidentiality and loyalty from my domestic staff.

_____7. I have at least two or three "screens" that keep people from me that I do not wish to see.

_____8. I fly in my own plane, the company plane, or the Concorde.

_____9. I know how to enroll my children in the preferred private schools.

_____10. I know how to host the parties that "key" people attend.

_____11. I am on the boards of at least two charities.

_____12. I know the hidden rules of the Junior League.

_____13. I have an artist that I support or buy hi/her work.

_____14. I know how to read a corporate financial statement and analyze my own financial statements.

The first point about this exercise is that if you fell mostly in middle class, the assumption is that everyone knows these things. However, if you did not know many of the items for the other classes, then the exercise points out how many of the hidden rules are taken for granted by a particular class which assumes they are given for everyone. What then are the hidden rules? This grid gives an overview of some of the major hidden rules among the classes of poverty, middle class, and wealth.

	POVERTY	MIDDLE CLASS	WEALTH
POSSESSIONS	People	Things	One of a kind objects, legacies, pedigrees
MONEY	To be used, spent	To be managed	To be conserved, invested
PERSON-ALITY	Is for entertainment. A sense of humor is highly valued.	Is for acquisition and stability. Achievement is highly valued.	Is for connections. Financial, political, social connections are highly valued.
SOCIAL EMPHASIS	Social inclusion of the people they like.	Emphasis is on self-governance and self-sufficiency.	Emphasis is on social exclusion.
FOOD	Key question: Did you have enough? Quantity important.	Key question: Did you like it? Quality important.	Key question: Was it presented well? Presentation important.
CLOTHING	Clothing valued for the individual style and expression of personality.	Clothing valued for its quality and acceptance into the norm of middle class. Label important.	Clothing valued for its artistic sense and expression. Designer important.

TIME	Present most important. Decisions made for the moment based on feelings or survival.	Future most important. Decisions made against future ramifications.	Traditions and past history most in..portant. Decisions partially made on basis of tradition /decorum.
EDUCATION	Valued and revered as an abstract but not as a reality.	Crucial for climbing success ladder and making money.	Necessary tradition for making and maintaining connections.
DESTINY	Believe in fate. Cannot do much to mitigate chance	Believe in choice. Can change the future with good choices now.	Noblesse oblige.
LANGUAGE	Casual register. Language is about survival.	Formal register. Language is about negotiation.	Formal register. Language is about connections.
FAMILY STRUCTURE	Tends to be matriarchal	Tends to be patriarchal	Depends on who has the money.
WORLD VIEW	Sees the world in terms of local setting	Sees the world in terms of national setting	Sees the world in terms of an international view.
LOVE	Love and acceptance unconditional, based upon whether or not an individual is liked.	Love and acceptance conditional and based largely on achievement.	Love and acceptance conditional and related to social standing and connections.
DRIVING FORCE	Survival, relationships and entertainment	Work and achievement	Financial, political, and social connections.

Several explanations and stories may help explain parts of the quiz and this chart. The bottom line or driving force against which decisions are made is important to note. For example, in one school district, the faculty had gotten together to buy a refrigerator for a family who did not have one. About three weeks later, the students were gone for a week. When the students returned the teachers asked where they had been. The answer was that the family had gone camping because they were so stressed. What had they used for money to go camping? The sale of the refrigerator - of course. The bottom line in generational poverty is entertainment and relationships. In middle class, the criteria against which almost all decisions are made relate to work and achievement. In wealth, it is the ramifications of the financial, social, and political connections that have the weight.

Being able physically to fight or have someone who is willing to fight for you is important to survival in poverty. Yet, in middle class, being able to use words as tools to negotiate conflict is crucial. Many times the fists are used in poverty because the words are neither available nor respected.

One of the biggest difficulties in getting out of poverty is managing money and just the general information base around money. How can you manage something you have never had? Money is seen in poverty as an expression of personality and is used for entertainment and relationships. The notion of using money for security is truly grounded in the middle and wealthy classes.

The question about using a knife as scissors in the quiz is put there to illustrate the lack of tools available to those in poverty. Tools in many ways are one of the identifiers of middle class - from the kitchen to the garage. Therefore, the notion of maintaining property and repairing items is dependent upon having tools. When they are not available, things are not repaired or maintained. Students do not have access to scissors, pens, paper, pencils, rulers, etc. which may be a part of an assignment.

One of the biggest differences among the classes is how the "world" is defined for them. Wealthy individuals view the international scene as their world. As one told me, "My favorite restaurant is in Brazil." Middle class tends to see the world in terms of a national picture while poverty sees the world in its immediate locale. Fourth grade poor students told us when they were writing to the prompt - *How is life in Houston different than in Baytown?* (Baytown is 20 minutes from Houston.) - "They don't have TV's in Houston."

In wealth to be introduced or accepted, one must have an individual already approved by that group make the introductions. Yet to stand back and not introduce yourself in a middle class setting is not the accepted norm. And in poverty it is not unusual to have a comment made about the individual before they are ever introduced.

The discussion could continue about hidden rules. The key point is that hidden rules govern so much of our immediate assessment of an individual and his/her capabilities. These are often the factors that keep an individual from moving upward in a career or even getting the position in the first place.

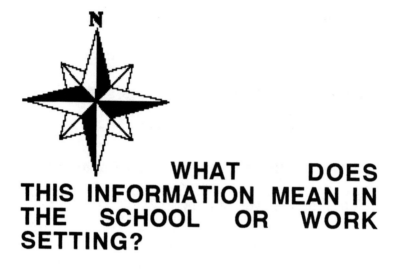

WHAT DOES THIS INFORMATION MEAN IN THE SCHOOL OR WORK SETTING?

* Assumptions made about individual's intelligence and approaches to the school and or work setting may be about his/her understanding of hidden rules.

* Students need to be taught the hidden rules of middle class - not in denigration of their own but rather as another set of rules that can be used if they so choose.

* Many of the attitudes that students and parents bring with them are an integral part of their culture and belief systems. Middle class solutions should not necessarily be imposed when other, more workable solutions, might be found.

* An understanding of the culture and values of poverty will lessen the anger educators may periodically feel when dealing with these students and parents.

*   Most of the students that I have talked to in poverty do not believe they are poor, even when they are on welfare. Most of the wealthy adults I have talked to do not believe they are wealthy; they will always cite someone who has more than they do.

✔CHAPTER FOUR: CHARACTERISTICS OF GENERATIONAL POVERTY

Generational poverty is defined as having been in poverty for at least two generations; however, the characteristics begin to surface much sooner than two generations if the family lives with others who are from generational poverty.

101

Situational poverty is defined as a lack of resources attributable to a particular event, i.e. a death, chronic illness, divorce, etc.

Generational poverty has its own culture, hidden rules, and belief systems. One of the key indicators of whether it is generational or situational poverty is the prevailing attitude. Often the attitude in generational poverty is that society owes them a living. In situational poverty the attitude is often one of pride and a refusal to accept charity. Individuals in situational poverty often bring more resources with them to the situation than those in generational poverty. Of particular importance is the use of formal register.

What then makes generational poverty so different from the middle class? How is it that school is such an unsatisfactory experience for many students from poverty? Several of these differences were mentioned in the last chapter on hidden rules. To examine the differences, a case study will be used.

CASE STUDY - (bold type indicates the narrator; plain type indicates comments from various participants. Names have been changed to protect the girl.)

103

WALTER (white male)

As the story would be told in poverty.....most probably by a relative or neighbor

Well, you know Walter got put away for 37 years.   Him being 48 and all.   He'll probably die in jail.   Just couldn't leave his hands off that 12 year old Susie. Dirty old man. Bodding's gonna whoop his tail. **Already did.   You know Bodding was waiting for him in jail and beat the living daylights out of him already.** In jail? **Yeah, Bodding got caught for possession.   Had $12,000 on him when they caught him**. Golly, wish I had been there to cash in!!!! (laughter) A man's gotta make a living! **Susie being blind and all - I can see why Bodding beat the daylights out of Walter.   Lucky he didn't get killed, old Walter is.** Too bad her momma is no good. **She started the whole thing!   Susie's momma goes over there and argues with Bodding**. Ain't they divorced? **Yea and she's got Walter working for her, repairing her house or something!** Or something, I bet. What she got in her house that's worth repairing? **Anyway she goes over to Bodding's house to take the lawnmower** - I reckon so as Walter can mow the yard?? I bet that's the first time old Walter has ever

104

broken a sweat! Reminds me of the time I saw Walter thinking about taking a job. All that thinking and he had to get drunk. He went to jail that time too - a felony as I recall- so many of those DWI's. Judge told him he was egregious. Walter said he wasn't greasy - he took a bath last week!!! (laughter) **Bodding and momma got in a battle so she tells Walter to take Susie with him.** Lordy - her elevator must not go all the way to the top!! Didn't she know about him gettin arrested for enticing a minor??? **And Susie blind and all. And she sends Susie with Walter?** She sure don't care about her babies. **Well, Walter's momma was there cause Walter lives with his momma seein as how he can't keep no job.** Ain't his other brother there? **Yea, and him 41 years old. That poor momma sure has her burdens to bear. And then her 30 year old daughter, Susie's momma, at home too. You know Susie's momma lost custody of her kids. Walter gets these videos, you know. Those adult videos. Heavy breathing!** (laughter) Some of those are more fun to listen to than to look at! (laughter) Some of those people are des-per-ate!! **Anyway, he puts those on and then carries Susie in his room and tells her she wants him and all his sex-u-al exploits with lesbians!!** Golly, he must be a loooooooooover. (laughter) He should be shot. I'd kill him if he did that to my kid!! **Then he lets his fingers do the walking.** Kinda like the yellow pages! (laughter) **I guess he didn't do anything with his "thang" according to Miss Rosie who went to that trial every day. And Susie begging him to stop so many times.** Probably couldn't do anything with it - that's why he needs to listen to the breathing! Pant! Pant! (laughter) What a no-count, low down creep. I'll pay Bodding to kill him!! **I hear tell that, according to Bodding, the only way Walter is coming out of jail is in a pine box.** Don't blame him, myself. **Yeah, Miss Rosie said Walter's momma said at the trial that the door to Walter's room was open and there ain't no way Walter could have done that. That she is a good Christian momma and she don't put up with that.** Oh Lordy, did God strike her dead on the spot or is she still alive??? I'd be afraid of being in eternal hell for telling a story like that! **Miss Rosie said that her 12 year old nephew who was there at the trial testified that the door was closed and his grandma told him to say it was open!!!!** Ooo! Oo! Oo! That poor baby tells the truth? His grandma gonna make him mis-er-a-ble!!! **And then Walter's momma tells that jury that she never allows those adult videos in her house, leastways not that she pays for it!!** (lots of laughter) I bet the judge bit on that one!! How is Walter gonna get videos except for her money? Mowing yards? (more laughter) No, I bet he saves his pennies!! (laughter) **All these years**

106

she has covered for Walter. Guess she just couldn't cover no more. Remember that time Walter got drunk and wrecked her car and she said she was driving? And she was at the hospital with a broken leg and when the judge asked her how she could be driving and in the hospital simultaneously? And she said that's just how it was - simultaneously - she had never felt so excited in her life? (laughter) Who turned Walter in? **Well it wasn't Susie's momma. She's busy with Skeeter, her new boyfriend. I hear he's something.** Remember that one boyfriend she had? Thought he was smart? **Speaking of smart - that Susie sure is. Her blind and all and she won the district spelling bee for the seventh grade this year. I hear she is in National Honor Society, whatever that is.** Wonder if it is kinda like the country club. Instead of playing golf, you just spell!!! (laughter) **Susie calls this friend of hers who tells her mother and they come and get her and take her to the police and hospital.** What's some wealthy woman doing - not minding her own business, that's for sure. **Well, it was a good thing for Susie, cause that Momma of hers sure ain't a good thing for Susie. She don't deserve a kid like Susie. She oughta be blind.** Ain't that the truth. Way I see it, she already is - look at Skeeter!! (lots of laughter)

(Actual court case heard in Houston, Texas during March 1995. Bold print indicates what came out in the trial; plain print indicates the kinds of comments that might be made by others in generational poverty.)

USING THIS CASE, WHICH CHARACTERISTICS OF GENERATIONAL POVERTY ARE PRESENT?

CHARACTERISTICS OF GENERATIONAL POVERTY

BACKGROUND "NOISE" - Almost always, the TV is always on, no matter what the circumstance. Conversation is participatory and more than one person talks at a time.

IMPORTANCE OF PERSONALITY - Individual personality is what one brings to the setting because money is not brought. The ability to entertain, tell stories, and have a sense of humor is highly valued.

IMPORTANCE OF ENTERTAINMENT - When one can only survive, then the respite from the survival is important. In fact, entertainment brings respite.

IMPORTANCE OF RELATIONSHIPS - One only has people upon which to rely and those relationships are important to survival. One often has favorites.

MATRIARCHAL STRUCTURE - The mother has the most powerful position in the society if she functions as a caretaker.

ORAL LANGUAGE TRADITION- Casual register is used for everything.

SURVIVAL ORIENTATION - Discussion of academic topics is generally not prized. There is little room for the abstract. Discussions center around people and relationships. A job is about making enough money to survive. A job is not about a career. " I was looking for a job when I found this one."

IDENTITY TIED TO LOVER/FIGHTER ROLE FOR MEN - The key issue for males is to be a "man." The rules are rigid and a man is expected to work hard physically, be a lover and a fighter.

IDENTITY TIED TO RESCUER/MARTYR ROLE FOR WOMEN - A "good" woman is expected to take care of and rescue her man and her children.

109

IMPORTANCE OF NON-VERBAL/KINESTHETIC COMMUNICATION - Touch is used to communicate a great deal as is space and non-verbal emotional information.

OWNERSHIP OF PEOPLE - People are possessions. There is a great deal of fear and comment about leaving the culture and "getting above your raisings."

NEGATIVE ORIENTATION - Failure at anything is the source of stories and numerous belittling comments.

DISCIPLINE - Punishment is about penance and forgiveness, not about change.

BELIEF IN FATE - Destiny and fate are the major tenants of the belief system. Choice is not considered.

POLARIZED THINKING - Options are not examined. Everything is polarized - it is one way or the other. These kinds of statements are common - "I quit." "I can't do it."

MATING DANCE - The mating dance is about using the body in a sexual way and verbally complimenting body parts. If you have few financial resources, the way you attract individuals of the opposite sex is with your body.

110

TIME - Time occurs only in the present. The future does not exist except as a word. Time is flexible and not measured. Time is often assigned on the basis of the emotional significance and not the actual measured time.

SENSE OF HUMOR - A sense of humor is highly valued as entertainment is one of the key aspects of poverty. Humor is almost always about people - either situations that people encounter or things people do to other people.

LACK OF ORDER/ORGANIZATION - Many of the homes/apartments are unkempt and cluttered. Devices for organization (files, planners, etc.) do not exist.

LIVES IN THE MOMENT - DOES NOT CONSIDER FUTURE RAMIFICATIONS - Being proactive, setting goals, planning ahead are not a part of generational poverty. Most of what occurs is reactive and in the moment. Future ramifications of present actions are not considered.

DEBRIEFING THE WALTER CASE STUDY

The Walter case study is an example of many of the issues in generational poverty. They all live together. Momma is still the most powerful position and these children are nearly 50. Momma will always make excuses for her children. After all, they are <u>her</u> children. The matriarchal structure and possession of people are there. She decides their guilt and punishment, not some outside authority. She leans on the self-righteous defense of being moral and Christian, but not in the middle class sense of Christianity. For her, it is simply one of unconditional love. Reality is the present - what can be persuaded and convinced in the present. Future ramifications are not considered by anyone. Entertainment is key - whether it is moral or not.

The neighbors' view of the situation gives more insight into the reality of generational poverty. While there is a deep distaste for sexual abuse of children, the story is really to make fun of Walter and his family as well as spread the news. Humor is used to cast aspersions on the character of Walter and his family. In many of these stories, aspersions would also be cast on the legal system and "rich lawyers." But there is an attitude of destiny or fate - what are you going to do about it? That's the way it is.

FAMILY PATTERNS IN GENERATIONAL POVERTY

One of the most confusing aspects in understanding generational poverty is the family patterns. In the middle class family, even with divorce, lineage is fairly easy to trace because of the legal documents. In generational poverty, many marital arrangements are common law. Marriage and divorce in a legal court is only important if there is property to distribute or custody of children. When you were never legally married to begin with and you have no property, why pay a lawyer for something you don't have, don't need, and don't have the money to purchase?

In the middle class, family trees tend to be drawn in this fashion.

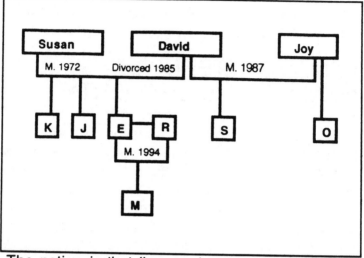

The notion is that lineage is traceable and that a linear pattern can be found.

In generational poverty, the mother is the center of the organization and the family radiates from that center. Although it can occur that the mother is uncertain of the biological father, most of the time, the father of the child is known. This is one pattern based on a real situation . (Names have been changed.)

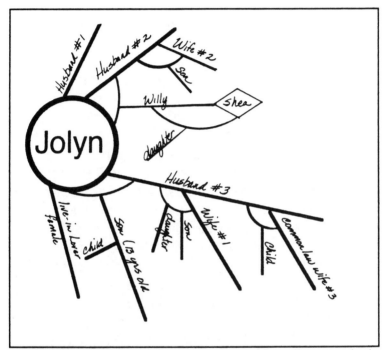

In this pattern, Jolyn has been legally married three times. Jolyn and Husband #1 had no children. Jolyn and Husband #2 had one child, Willy. They divorced. Husband #2 eventually married the woman he lived with for several years and they had a child together. She also had a son from a previous marriage. Willy has a common law wife, Shea; Shea and Willy have a daughter. Jolyn and Husband #3 lived together several years before they were married and they have a son named M.J. When M.J. was 13 he had a child with another 13 year old girl but that child lives with the girl's mother. Husband #3 and Jolyn divorced;

115

Jolyn is now living with another woman. Husband #3 is living with a younger woman who is pregnant with his child.

The mother is always at the center, although she may have multiple relationships. Many of her children will have multiple relationships which may or may not produce children. The basic pattern is the mother at the center, with nearly everyone having multiple relationships, some legal and some not. Eventually the relationships become intertwined. It would not be out of the question that your sister's third husband became your brother's ex-wife's live-in boyfriend. Also in this pattern are children born to children out of wedlock; this child is often raised by the grandmother as one of her own children. For example, the oldest daughter has a child at fourteen. This baby becomes the youngest child in the existing family . The oldest daughter who is actually the mother of the child is referred to as her sister and the relationship is a sibling one, not a mother-daughter one.

But the mother or maternal grandmother tends to keep her biological children. Because of the violence in poverty, death is a part of the family history. But it is also a part of the family present because the dead person plays such a role in the memories of the family. It is important to note when dealing with the family patterns who is alive and who is dead because in the discussions, they are often still living (unless you, the listener, know differently).

Often in the stories that are brought to school officials, the individual will tell the story in the episodic random manner of the casual register story structure. Key individuals are often not referred to during the story because it is not a part of the story structure to make reference to them. **THE MOST IMPORTANT PARTS TO UNDERSTANDING THE STORY ARE OFTEN THE OMISSIONS.** For example, when someone says, "He left, " you can pretty much predict who "he" will go stay with when there is trouble. If he is having trouble with his mother, he will go stay with an ex-wife or a girlfriend. If he is having trouble with his current wife, he will go stay with his mother. Women tend to go stay with their sisters and sometimes their mothers. Whether or not a mother or ex-wife is mentioned in the story, if the family is in generational poverty, you can be fairly certain that these are key players. You can also be fairly certain that the males are in and out, sometimes present, sometimes not, but not in any predictable pattern. You can also know that as the male temporarily or permanently changes residences, the allegiances will change also.

Within these families, there also tends to be multiple internal feuds. Allegiances change overnight; favoritism is a way of life. **So who children go to stay with after school, who**

117

stays with whom when there is trouble, and who is available to deal with school issues is dependent upon the current alliances and relationships at that moment. For example, Ned comes home drunk and beats up his wife, Susan. She calls the police and escapes with the three kids to her mother's house. He goes to his mother's because his mother arranges to get him out of jail. His mother is not speaking to Susan because she called the cops on him and put him in jail. But Ned's mother usually keeps his kids after school until Susan gets home. Now it is Monday and Susan doesn't have any place to send the kids. So she tells them to go her mother's house after school which means they must go on a different bus because she doesn't know if Ned will show up at the house and be waiting for her. On Tuesday, the kids go to Susan's mom's house. But on Wednesday, Ned's mom calls Susan and tells her that that no-good Ned got drunk last night and she kicked him out of her house. So now, Susan and Ned's mom are good friends and Ned is on the hot seat. So Ned goes to his ex-wife, Jackie's house, because last week she decided she had had enough of Jerry and she was very glad to see Ned. .... And so the story continues.

The key roles in these families are the fighter/lover; the caretaker/rescuer; the worker; the storyteller; and the "keeper of the soul", i.e. the dispenser of penance and forgiveness. The family patterns in generational poverty are different than in the middle class. **The roles, the multiple relationships, the nature of the male identity, the ever-changing allegiances, the favoritism, and the matriarchial structure make a different pattern.**

HOW THESE CHARACTERISTICS SURFACE WITH ADULTS AND STUDENTS FROM POVERTY
They..

- get mad and quit the job. If they do not like the boss/teacher, they will quit. The emphasis is on the current feeling, not the long term ramifications.

- will work hard if they like you.

- Do not use conflict resolution skills. Prefer to settle issues in verbal or physical assaults.

- Use survival language. Tend to operate out of casual register.

- Are not emotionally reserved when angry. Tend to say exactly what is on their mind.

119

- Have an extreme freedom of speech, enjoy a sense of humor, use the personality to entertain, have a love of stories about people.

- Are extremely independent. Will not take kindly to the "parent" voice. If their full cooperation is sought, boss/employer needs to use the "adult" voice.

- Periodically need time off or late arrival due to family emergencies.

-Need emotional warmth from colleagues/boss/teacher(s) in order to feel comfortable.

- Require a level of integrity from the management. Have an active distrust of organizations and the people who represent the organizations. See organizations as basically dishonest.

- Exhibit a possessiveness about the people they really like.

- Need a greater amount of "space" to allow for the uniqueness of their personalities.

- Show favoritism for certain people and give them preferential treatment.

ALSO....

- Men socialize with men and women with women. Men tend to have two social outlets - bars and work. Women with children tend to stay at home and only have other female relatives for friends, unless they work. Men tend to be loners in any other social setting and avoid those social settings. When a man and a woman are together, it is usually about a private relationship.

- A real man is ruggedly good-looking, is a lover, can physically fight, works hard, takes no crap.

- A real woman takes care of her man by feeding him.

TO NOTE

- In generational poverty, the primary role of a real man is to physically work hard, be a fighter and a lover. In the middle class, a real man is a provider. If you follow the ramifications of a male identify as one who is a fighter and a lover, then you can understand why the male who takes this identify of a fighter and lover as his own cannot have a stable life. Of the three responses to life - to flee, flow, or fight - he can only fight or flee. So when the stress gets high, he fights and flees the law or loves and flees his home - either way he is gone. When the

heat dies down, he returns - to an initial welcome and then fights. The cycle begins again.

HOW THESE CHARACTERISTICS SURFACE AT SCHOOL

Students....

*   are extremely disorganized, frequently loose papers, don't have signatures, etc.

* bring many reasons why something is missing, or the paper is gone, etc.

* don't do homework.

* are physically aggressive.

* like to entertain.

* only see part of what is on the page.

* only do a part of the assignment.

* can't seem to get started (no procedural self talk)

* cannot monitor their own behavior.

* laugh when they are disciplined.

* decide whether they will work or not in your class based on whether they like you.

* tell stories in the casual register structure.

* don't know or use middle class courtesies.

* dislike authority.

* talk back and are extremely participatory.

GENERATIONAL POVERTY

One of the reasons it is getting more and more difficult to conduct school as we have in the past is that the students who bring the middle class culture with them are decreasing in numbers and the students who bring the poverty culture with them are increasing in numbers. As in any demographic switch, the prevailing rules and policies eventually give way to the group with the largest numbers.

In order to better serve these students, the next several chapters have ideas about ways in which we can work with students and adults. But to

123

do so, we must fundamentally rethink the notions we have traditionally assigned to relationships and achievement.

WHAT DOES THIS INFORMATION MEAN IN THE SCHOOL OR WORK SETTING?

*   An **education** is the key to getting out of and staying out of generational poverty. Individuals leave poverty for one of four reasons: a goal or vision or something they want to be or have; a situation that is so painful that anything would be better; someone who "sponsors" them, i.e. an educator or spouse or mentor or role model who shows them a way or convinces them that they could live differently; or a specific talent or ability provides an opportunity for them.

* Being in poverty is rarely about a lack of intelligence or ability.

* Many individuals stay in poverty because they do not know there is a choice and if they do know that, have no one to teach them hidden rules or provide resources.

* Schools are the only place where students can learn the choices and rules of the middle class.

✔ CHAPTER FIVE: ROLE MODELS AND EMOTIONAL RESOURCES

To understand the importance of role models and their part in the development of emotional resources, one must first briefly look at the notion of functional and dysfunctional systems. The following definitions will be used:

A *SYSTEM* IS A GROUP IN WHICH INDIVIDUALS HAVE RULES, ROLES, AND RELATIONSHIPS.

DYSFUNCTIONAL IS THE EXTENT TO WHICH AN INDIVIDUAL CANNOT GET HIS/HER NEEDS MET WITHIN A SYSTEM.

All systems are to some extent dysfunctional. A system is not equally functional or dysfunctional for each individual within a given system. The extent to which an individual must give up meeting his/her needs in order to meet the needs of another individual is the extent to which the situation is dysfunctional.

ELLIE

Michael Dumont (1994) gives in detail a case study of a girl named Ellie. Her mother, Victoria, is bedridden with multiple sclerosis and her father, Larry, is a small storekeeper. Victoria, in her rage at the disease and her distrust of Larry, attempts suicide when Ellie is nine years old. It is Ellie's job each day when she comes home from school to count her mother's pills to make certain they are all there, and to check to see if her mother is alive. Ellie tells Mr. Dumont that the worst part of her day is when she comes home from school and must check on her mother's well-being. When he tells Ellie that she is smart and asks her what she wants to be, she tells him she would like to be a secretary. At 13, Ellie becomes pregnant and drops out of school.

128

The situation is extremely **dysfunctional** for Ellie because she must sublimate her needs to address the needs of her mother. In order for Ellie to have an appropriate emotional developmental process, she needs to be a child, then an adolescent, then an adult. But by forcing her to take on an adult role earlier, she must in essence put her emotional development on hold while she functions in an adult role. Therefore, for the rest of her life, Ellie will seek to have her emotional needs met that were not met during her childhood. She will not have the emotional resources and stamina necessary to function as an interdependent adult.

DEPENDENCE

INDEPENDENCE

INTERDEPENDENCE

To become a fully functioning adult, developmentally one moves from being dependent to being independent to being interdependent. Stephen Covey (1989) refers to it as *the maturity continuum*, and Bradshaw (1988) refers to it *as becoming whole.* Regardless of the terminology it simply means moving from being dependent on others to being able to work together with other adults, each independent of the other , but jointly, as equal partners.

Simply put, an individual operating in a dysfunctional setting is often forced to take an adult role early, and then as an adult, is literally caught between being dependent and independent. So one will see this fierce independence coupled with a crippling dependence that weakens the individual to the point that she/he has few emotional resources. This roller coaster ride back and forth between dependence and independence takes a heavy toll. Bradshaw and others refer to this movement between dependence and independence as *co-dependency.*

As this case study illustrates, the emotional resources come in part from the role models who are present for the child. When the appropriate

131

role models are present, the child can go through the developmental stages at appropriate times and build emotional resources. Emotional resources are built in this fashion: the child watches the adult for emotional responses to a given situation and notes the continuum of behaviors that go with those responses. In Ellie's situation, her mother's response to her husband's infidelity was to create an even greater level of dependence, and to use the emotional ploy of guilt to manipulate Ellie. So what does Ellie do when she gets old enough? She creates a level of dependence on others as well i.e. through pregnancies and going on welfare.

A child may decide that the role model responses are not appropriate. Often what occurs then is that the child selects the opposite extreme

from which to operate. What is problematic for the

child is simply that what is "normal" - what is an

appropriate adult response is rarely observable.

So the child is forced to guess at what "normal" or

appropriate is.

WHY WOULD EMOTIONAL RESOURCES HAVE SUCH IMPORTANCE IN SCHOOL AND AT WORK?

EMOTIONAL RESPONSES DICTATE BEHAVIOR AND, EVENTUALLY, DETERMINE ACHIEVEMENT.

Futhermore, In order to move from poverty to middle class or from middle class to wealth, one must trade off relationships for achievement. To do this, one must have emotional resources and stamina.

133

An **emotional memory bank** is defined as the emotions that are accessed habitually and "feel right." When a relationship is traded off for achievement, the emotional memory bank must be held in abeyance until the new "feel right" feeling can be obtained. That process sometimes take years. The driving force behind an individual holding the emotional memory bank in abeyance is usually one of four things: (1) the current situation is too painful for the individual to stay; (2) a compelling goal or vision of the future drives the individual; (3) a talent or skill takes the individual into new surroundings; (4) a spouse or mentor provides an emotional comfort level while the individual learns the new skills/knowledge.

Emotional resources and stamina allow the individual to live with other feelings than those in the emotional memory bank. This allowance provides the individual the opportunity to seek options and examine other possibilities. As the case study shows, Ellie stays with her emotional memory bank and creates situations that "feel right.

HOW DO YOU PROVIDE EMOTIONAL RESOURCES WHEN THE STUDENT HAS NOT HAD ACCESS TO APPROPRIATE ROLE MODELS?

1. Through support systems.

2. By using appropriate discipline strategies and approaches.

3. By establishing long term relationships (apprenticeships, mentorships) with adults who are appropriate.

4. By teaching the hidden rules.

5. By identifying options.

6. By increasing individual's achievement level through appropriate instruction.

7. By teaching goal setting.

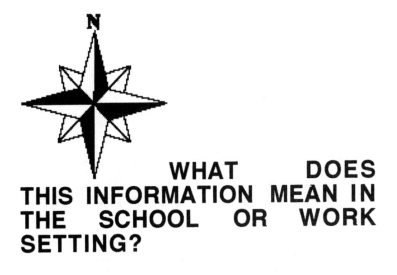

WHAT DOES THIS INFORMATION MEAN IN THE SCHOOL OR WORK SETTING?

* Schools need to establish schedules and instructional arrangements which allows students to stay with the same teachers for three or more years.

* Teachers and administrators are much more important as role models than has previously been addressed.

* The development of emotional resources is crucial to student success. The greatest free resource available to schools is the role modeling provided by teachers and administrators and staff.

☑ CHAPTER SIX: SUPPORT SYSTEMS

Support systems are the friends, family and backup resources that can be accessed in times of need.

COPING STRATEGIES

OPTIONS DURING PROBLEM SOLVING

INFORMATION & KNOW-HOW

TEMPORARY RELIEF

CONNECTIONS - PEOPLE/RESOURCES

POSITIVE SELF-TALK   PROCEDURAL SELF-TALK

1. COPING STRATEGIES

Coping strategies are the ways in which one copes with daily living - the disappointments, the tragedies, the triumphs. Coping strategies are ways to think about things, attitudes, self-talk, strategies for resolving conflicts, solving problems, and avoiding needless conflicts. Coping strategies are ways of approaching tasks, setting priorities, and determining what one can live with and what one can live without.

2. OPTIONS DURING PROBLEM SOLVING

Options are all the ways to solve a problem. Even very capable adults often talk over a problem with another adult just in order to see other options they have not considered.

139

3. INFORMATION AND KNOW HOW

This is a key aspect of a support system. When a child has homework, who in the support system knows enough math to help the child? Who knows the research process? Who knows the ropes for going to college or getting a new car loan? Who knows how to talk to the insurance agent so the situation can be clarified? Who knows how to negotiate difficult situations with a teacher and come to a resolution? Who understands the court system? the school system? Information and know how are crucial to success.

4. TEMPORARY RELIEF FROM EMOTIONAL, MENTAL, FINANCIAL, AND/OR TIME CONSTRAINTS

140

When you are upset, who provides relief for you? When you are not sure how you will get everything finished, who helps you? Who takes your children when you are desperate for a break? These people are all part of a support system.

5. **CONNECTIONS TO OTHER PEOPLE AND RESOURCES**

When you do not have the information and know how, who are the people you turn to for assistance? Those people are your connections. Connections to people and resources are an integral part of a healthy support system.

141

6. POSITIVE SELF-TALK

Everyone has a little voice inside his/her head that talks to him/her all the time. This little voice gives encouraging messages.   These encouraging messages help one finish tasks, complete projects, and get through difficult situations. If an individual does not listen to this encouraging little voice, the success rate is much lower.

7. PROCEDURAL SELF-TALK

Procedural self-talk is the voice that talks an individual through a task.   It is key to success. Many individuals in poverty have a very limited support system -- particularly missing is procedural self-talk.   Many tasks are never finished.   In numerous dealings with students, the self-talk is simply not available to the student.

The following case study identifies what aspects of a support system would be beneficial to a student and promote success.

FRIENDS

FAMILY

BACKUP   RESOURCES

You are a high school social studies teacher in inner city Houston. One of your students, LaKeitha, was so rude in your tenth grade class that you told her she could not return until you had a conversation with her mother. She calls her mother and tells you that the mother will be there at 7:30

143

a.m. the next day to meet with you. You are at school the next morning at 7:15 a.m. LaKeitha's mother never shows up.

The next day, LaKeitha is waiting for you before school. She is crying. She apologizes profusely for her behavior and tells you the following. Her dad is in jail. She is the oldest of five children. Her mother works two jobs and LaKeitha works from 5:00 - 9:00 p.m. at Burger King every day to bring in money. Yesterday, her mother was on her way to school to see you but she got stopped by the police for an expired inspection sticker, and because she did not have a driver's license, was put in jail. Her mother is in jail now as well and she is all alone with the children. She is fifteen years old.

LaKeitha asks to be back in your class and she asks you to help get her mother out of jail.

WHAT SUPPORT SYSTEMS CAN BE ACCESSED TO HELP LAKEITHA?

Here is a sample list of the support systems some schools use to help students.

SUPPORT SYSTEMS SCHOOLS USE

1. **School wide homework support** - A very successful middle school in Texas schedules the last 45 minutes of every day for homework support. Students who did not get their homework done must go to the cafeteria where individuals are available to help them with their homework. The students must stay until their homework is finished. They have arranged for a late bus run to take students home. Many poor students do not have access to adults who have the knowledge base to help them with homework. The school has built this into the school day. Another middle school has arranged for students to have two sets of textbooks - one set at home and one at school. This school

does not have lockers. The school has eliminated several problems and has also provided support for students.

2. **Supplemental school wide reading programs** - Many schools have gone to the concept of an Accelerated Reader program, using a computer based management program which provides tests for students to take over the book(s) they have read. Students will be encouraged to read more because the programs are designed so students are not penalized for what their parents do not know or cannot provide for them.

3. **Keeping students with the same teacher(s) for two to three years** or having a

school within a school is another one. Both of these concepts are designed to build longer term relationships between teachers and students. Considerably less time is wasted at the beginning of the year establishing   relationships with the students and their parents.

4. Teaching coping strategies can be done in several ways. One is to address each issue as a student needs assistance.   Many schools have small groups which meet with the counselor, principal, or a teacher during lunch to work on coping strategies in a number of areas.   This ongoing group support allows students to discuss issues and ways to deal with those issues.   For example, one elementary school divided all of its

sixth graders into groups of 8. Then they took these

students and met with them for four weeks, twice a

week over lunch, to discuss the issues they would

face the next year when they went on to junior high

school.   Another school has a similar group of

students meet who are physically aggressive and

the discussion centers around ways to lessen the

aggression at school.   Advisory groups are yet

another way to address issues.

5.   **School wide scheduling** that subgroups

students by skill for reading and math can be a way

of   providing   support.   One   concern   with

heterogeneous grouping is the difficulty for the

teacher to address all of the diverse instructional needs in the classroom simultaneously. One elementary school scheduled the hour for math at the same time in grades 1 through 3 as well as 4 through 6. Students were then pretested and moved to the appropriate group for that particular unit of instruction. Within two years, the math scores in that building made a considerable gain.

6. **Parent training and contact through video** is invaluable, particularly in poor communities. One characteristic of the poor communities is that virtually everyone has a VCR because of the value placed on entertainment. A principal in Illinois who had 95% of his parents on

welfare started a very successful program of parental education and contact through videos. Each teacher in the building made a fifteen minute videotape. During that fifteen minutes, the teacher gave a personal introduction, gave an overview of the instruction for the year, identified the expectations of the class, and encouraged the parents to visit or call. Five copies of each video were made and during the first month of school each student could take a copy home and have an adult view the video. This was very successful for several reasons: (1) parents who were not literate could understand; (2) it provided a kinesthetic view and feel for the teacher; (3) the parent was not dependent upon transportation to have a contact with the school; (4) it prevented unnecessary miscommunications early in the year. It is a low cost intervention and other short videos could be made for parents about appropriate discipline, etc.

7. **The direct teaching of classroom survival skills** makes a difference according to the research. What are classroom survival skills? Many of these skills are referred to as study skills but there are also the cognitive strategies which are discussed in Chapter 8 on Instruction. These include such simple hidden rules as how to stay in your seat, how to participate appropriately, where to put your things, etc.

8.   Requiring daily goal setting and procedural self-talk would move many of these students light years ahead. In the beginning goal setting would focus on what a student wants to accomplish by the end of each day and by the end of a week. Goals would be in writing. At the end of the day, five minutes would need to be taken with the class to see if the goals were met or not. Procedural self-talk would begin in the written form first and would need to be assisted. Procedural self-talk only has value when tied to a specific task. Procedures vary with tasks.

9. **Team interventions** are a way to provide support to students. This happens when all the teachers of a student meet with the parents to make

a plan for helping that student be more successful.

This works as long as the intervention with the parents is positive and supportive.

DEBRIEFING THE CASE STUDY

LAKEITHA

One of LaKeitha's issues is simply time. She doesn't have any extra time. One of the things the teacher can have LaKeitha do is identify when, given her schedule, she can get things done. The teacher needs to provide flexibility for her to finish her assignments (maybe an extra day) and be flexible about the interruptions that will be a part of her life. The teacher can also give LaKeitha phone numbers and addresses of organizations (churches, social agencies, etc) who can help provide some relief to her mentally, emotionally, financially and physically. Someone needs to spend five minutes with LaKeitha explaining how to access adult voice, and how to use that voice will help her negotiate her difficulties with authority figures and be a better caretaker of her siblings. Certainly, of great importance, is the acceptance and understanding of her situation from the teacher.

153

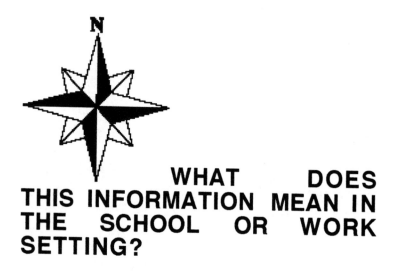

WHAT DOES THIS INFORMATION MEAN IN THE SCHOOL OR WORK SETTING?

* By reorganizing the school day and schedule, and often by making minor adjustments, support systems can be built into the school day without additional cost.

* Support systems need to include the teaching of procedural self-talk, positive self-talk, planning, goal setting, coping strategies, appropriate relationships, options during problem-solving, access to information and know-how, and connections to additional resources.

154

✓ CHAPTER SEVEN: DISCIPLINE

In poverty, discipline is about penance and forgiveness. Because love is unconditional and because the time frame is the present, the notion that discipline should be instructive and change behavior is not a part of the culture in generational poverty. In matriarchial, generational poverty, the mother has the most powerful position and is in some ways, "keeper of the soul." So she dispenses the judgments, determines the amount and price of penance, and gives forgiveness. When forgiveness is granted, behaviors and activities return to the way it was before the incident.

It is important to note that the approach advocated in this book to discipline is to teach a separate set of behaviors. MANY OF THE BEHAVIORS STUDENTS BRING TO SCHOOL ARE NECESSARY TO HELP THEM SURVIVE OUTSIDE OF SCHOOL. Just as students learn and many use different rules depending on the Nintendo game they are playing, they also need to learn to use the various different rules necessary to be successful in school settings and circumstances.. If poor students do not know how to fight physically, they are going to be in danger on the streets. But if that is their only method for resolving a problem, then they cannot be successful in school.

The culture of poverty does not provide for success in middle class because middle class to a large extent requires the self-governance of behavior. To be successful in work and in school requires the self-governance of behavior. What then do schools need to do to teach appropriate behavior?

STRUCTURE AND CHOICE

The two anchors of any effective discipline program which moves students to self-governance are structure and choice. The program must clearly outline the expected behaviors and the consequences of not choosing those behaviors. The program must also emphasize that the individual always has a choice - to follow or not to follow the expected behaviors. With each choice then comes consequence - either

158

desirable or not desirable.   Many discipline workshops use this approach and are available to schools.

When the focus is "I'll tell you what to do and when"   the student can never move from dependence to independence, but is always at the level of dependence.

BEHAVIOR ANALYSIS

Mentally   or in writing, the teacher or administrator must first answer certain questions about the behavior.

159

BEHAVIOR ANALYSIS

1. What sort of behaviors does a child need to be successful?

2. Does the child have the resources to develop those behaviors?

3. Will it help to contact parent(s)? Are resources available through them? What resources are available through the school/district?

4. How will behaviors be taught?

5. What are other choices the child could make?

6. What will help the child repeat the successful behavior?

When these questions are answered, they lead to the strategies which will most help the student.

This chart indicates possible explanations of behaviors and possible interventions.

BEHAVIOR RELATED TO POVERTY

RELATED INTERVENTION

BEHAVIOR RELATED TO POVERTY	INTERVENTION
LAUGHS WHEN DISCIPLINED - a way to save face in matriarchial poverty	Understand the reason for the behavior. Tell the student three or four other behaviors that would be more appropriate.
ARGUES LOUDLY WITH THE TEACHER -poverty is participatory and the culture has a distrust of authority. Sees the system as inherently dishonest and unfair.	Don't argue with the student. Use the four part sheet in the this chapter and make students write the answers to the questions. Model respect for students.
ANGRY RESPONSE - anger is based on fear. Question what the fear is - loss of face?	Respond in the adult voice. When student cools down, discuss other responses student could have used.
INAPPROPRIATE OR VULGAR COMMENTS- Reliance on casual register, may not know formal register.	Make student generate or teach student other phrases that could be used to say the same thing.
PHYSICALLY FIGHTS - necessary to survive in	Stress that fighting is unacceptable in school.

poverty. Only knows the language of survival. Does not have language or belief system to use conflict resolution. Sees himself as less than a man or woman if he/she does not fight.

Examine other options that the student could live with at school other than fighting. One option is not to settle the business at school, for example.

HANDS ALWAYS ON SOMEONE ELSE - poverty has a heavy reliance on non-verbal data and touch.

Allow them to draw or doodle. Have them hold their hands behind their backs when in line or standing. Give them as much to do with their hands as is possible in a constructive way.

CANNOT FOLLOW DIRECTIONS - little procedural memory used in poverty. Sequence not used or valued.

Write steps on the board. Have them write at the top of the paper the steps needed to finish the task. Have them practice procedural self-talk.

EXTREMELY DISORGANIZED - lack of planning, scheduling, or prioritizing skills. Not taught in poverty. Also, probably does not have a place to put things at home so that they can be found.

Teach a simple color coded method of organization in the classroom. Use the five finger method for memory at the end of the day. Make each student give a plan for organization.

ONLY COMPLETES PART OF A TASK -no

Write on the board all the parts of the task. Make

162

procedural self-talk. Does not "see" the whole task.

students check off each part when finished.

DISRESPECTFUL TO TEACHER - has a lack of respect for authority and the system. May not know any adults worthy of respect.

Tell the student that is not a choice. Identify for the student the correct voice tone and word choice that is acceptable. This allows the student to practice.

HARMS OTHER STUDENTS - VERBALLY OR PHYSICALLY - may be a way of life. Probably a way to buy space or distance. May have become an habitual response. Poverty tends to address issues in the negative.

Tell the student that approach is not a choice. Have the student generate other options that are a choice at school. Give the student verbal phrases that can be used instead of the one(s) used.

CHEATS OR STEALS - indicative of weak support system, weak role models/emotional resources. May indicate extreme financial need. May indicate no instruction/guidance during formative years.

Use metaphor story to find the reason or need the cheating or stealing met. Address the reason or need. Stress that the behavior is illegal and not a choice at school.

CONSTANTLY TALKS - poverty is very participatory.

Have students write all questions and responses on a notecard two days a week. Tell a student he/she gets five comments a day. Build participatory activities into the lesson.

163

PARTICIPATION OF THE STUDENT

While the teacher or administrator is analyzing, the student must analyze as well. To help the student do so, this four part questionnaire is given to the student for completion. This has been used with students as young as second semester first grade. Students have the most difficulty with question number three. Basically, they see no other choices available than the one they have made.

In going over the sheet with the student, it is important to discuss other choices that could have been made. Students often only know one choice. They do not have access to another way to deal with the situation. For example, if I slam my finger in the car door, I can cry, cuss, hit the car, be silent, kick the tire, laugh, stoically open the car door, groan, etc.

NAME:

1. **WHAT DID YOU DO?**

2. **WHY DID YOU DO THAT?**

3. **LIST 4 OTHER THINGS YOU COULD HAVE DONE.**

    1.

    2.

    3.

    4.

4. **WHAT WILL YOU DO NEXT TIME?**

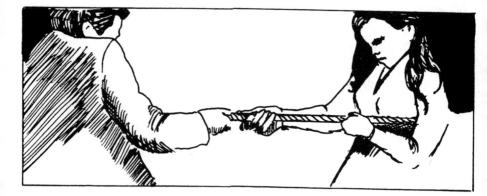

THE LANGUAGE OF NEGOTIATION

One of the bigger issues with students from poverty is the fact that many children in poverty must function as their own parents. They parent themselves and others - often younger siblings. In many instances, they also act as the parent to the adult in the household.

Inside everyone's head are internal voices which guide the individual. These three voices are referred to as the child voice, the adult voice, and the parent voice. It has been my observation that individuals who have become their own parent quite young do not have an internal adult voice. They have a child voice and a parent voice, but not an adult voice.

An internal adult voice allows for negotiation. This voice provides the language of negotiation and allows issues to be examined in a non-threatening way.

Educators tend to speak to students in a parent voice, particularly in discipline situations. To the student who is already functioning as a parent, this is unbearable. Almost immediately, the incident is exacerbated beyond the original happening. The tendency is for educators to use the parent voice with poor parents is based on the assumption that a lack of resources must indicate a lack of intelligence. Poor parents are extremely offended by this.

When the parent voice is used with a student who is already a parent in many ways, the outcome is anger. The student is angry because anger is based on fear. What the parent voice forces the student to do is either use the child voice or use the parent voice. If the student uses the parent voice, the student will get in trouble. If the student uses the child voice, he/she will feel helpless and therefore at the mercy of the adult. Many students chose to use the parent voice because it is less frightening than memories connected with being helpless.

Part of the reality of poverty is the language of survival. There are simply not enough resources to engage in a discussion of them. For example, if there are five hot dogs and five people, the distribution of the food is fairly clear. The condiments for the hot dogs are going to be limited so the discussion will be fairly limited as well. Contrast that, for example, with a middle class household where the discussion will be about how many hot dogs, what should go on the hot dog, how much of each ingredient, etc. So the ability to see options and to negotiate among those options is not well developed.

To teach students to use the "language of negotiation" one must first teach them the phrases they can use. Especially, beginning in grade four, have them use the "adult" voice in discussions. Direct teach the notion of an adult voice and give them phrases to use. Make them tally each time they use a phrase from the "adult" voice. There will be laughter. However, over time, if the teacher also models that voice in interactions with students, one will hear more of those kinds of questions and statements.

In addition to this strategy, several staff development programs are available to teach peer negotiation. It is important that as a part of the negotiation, the culture of origin is not denigrated, but rather the ability to negotiate is seen as a survival skill for the work and school setting.

THREE VOICES

---

*   THE CHILD VOICE- Defensive, victimized, emotional, whining, losing mentality, strong negative, non-verbal

---

~   Quit picking on me.
~   You don't love me.
~   You want me to leave.
~   Nobody likes (loves) me.
~   I hate you.
~   You are ugly.
~   You make me sick.
~   It's your fault.
~   Don't blame me.
~   She, he, ... did it.
~   You make me mad.
~   You make me do it.

*   *The child voice is also playful, spontaneous, curious, etc. These phrases listed occur in conflict or manipulative situations and impede resolution.*

THREE VOICES

THE ADULT VOICE -Non-judgmental, free of negative non-verbal, factual, often in question format, attitude of win-win.

~ In what ways could this be resolved?

~ What criteria will be used to determine the effectiveness, quality of ....

~ I would like to recommend ....

~ What are choices in this situation?

~ I am comfortable (uncomfortable) with ....

~ Options that could be considered are................

~ For me to be comfortable, I need the following things to occur ....

~ These are the consequences of that choice / action ....

~ We agree to disagree.

THREE VOICES

---

* ** THE PARENT VOICE - Authoritative, directive, judgmental, evaluative, win-lose mentality, advising, (sometimes threatening, demanding, punitive)

~ You should not (should) do that.
~ It is wrong (right)to do that
....
~ I would advise you to ....
~ That's stupid, immature, out of line, ridiculous
~ Life's not fair. Get busy.
~ You are good, bad, worthless, beautiful (any judgmental, evaluative comment)
~ You do as I say.
~ If you weren't so ...., this wouldn't happen to you.

*   *The parent voice can also be very loving and supportive. The phrases listed here occur during conflict and impede resolution*

**   *The internal parent voice can create shame and guilt.*

171

USING METAPHOR STORIES

Another technique for working with students and adults is to use a metaphor story. A metaphor story will help an individual voice issues that affect subsequent actions.

A metaphor story does not have any proper names in it and goes like this. For example, a student keeps going to the nurse's office two or three times a week. There is nothing wrong with her. Yet she keeps going. Adult says to Jennifer, the girl, "Jennifer, I am going to tell a story and I need you to help me. It is about a fourth grade girl much like yourself. I need you to help me tell the

172

story because I am not in the fourth grade. Once upon a time, there was a girl who went to the nurse's office. Why did the girl go to the nurse's office? *(Because she thought there was something wrong with her.)* So the girl went to the nurse's office because she thought there was something wrong with her. Did the nurse find anything wrong with her? *(No, the nurse did not.)* So the nurse did not find anything wrong with her, yet the girl kept going to the nurse. Why did the girl keep going to the nurse? *(Because she thought there was something wrong with her.)* So the girl thought something was wrong with her. Why did the girl think there was something wrong with her? *(She saw a TV show.....)*"

The story continues until the reason for the behavior is found and then the story needs to end on a positive note. "So she went to the doctor and he gave her tests and found that she was ok."

This is an actual case and what came out in the story was that Jennifer had seen a TV show in which a girl her age had died suddenly and had never known she was ill. Her parents took her to the doctor, he ran tests, and he told her she was fine, so she did not go to the nurse's office anymore.

A metaphor story is to be used one-on-one when there is a need to understand the existing behavior and motivate the student to the appropriate behavior.

TEACHING HIDDEN RULES

For example, if a student from poverty laughs when he is disciplined, the teacher needs to say, "Do you use the same rules to play all Nintendo games? No, you don't because you would lose. The same is true at school. There are street rules and there are school rules. Each set of rules helps you be successful where you are. So, at school, laughing when disciplined is not a choice. It does not help you to be successful. It only buys you more trouble. Keep a straight face and look contrite, even if you don't feel that way."

This is an example of teaching a hidden rule. It can even be more straightforward with older students. "Look, there are hidden rules on the streets and hidden rules at school. What are they?"

After the discussion, detail the rules that make the student successful where they are.

WHAT DOES THIS INFORMATION MEAN IN THE SCHOOL OR WORK SETTING?

* Students from poverty need to have at least two sets of behaviors from which to choose -- one for the street and one for school and work.

* The purpose of discipline should be to promote successful behaviors at school.

* Teaching students to use the adult voice, i.e. the language of negotiation, is important for success in and out of school and can become an alternative to physical aggression.

175

* Structure and choice need to be a part of the discipline approach.

* Discipline should be a form of instruction.

✓ CHAPTER EIGHT: INSTRUCTION IMPROVING ACHIEVEMENT

One of the overriding purposes of this book is to improve the achievement of students from poverty. **Low achievement is closely correlated with lack of resources and numerous studies have documented the correlation between low socio-economic status and low achievement.** (Hodgkinson, 1995) To improve achievement, however, we will need to rethink our instruction and instructional arrangements.

1. TRADITIONAL NOTIONS OF INTELLIGENCE

For years and still very prevalent is the notion that ;all intelligence is inherited. In fact, the book, The Bell Curve, purports that individuals in poverty have on the average an IQ of nine points lower than individuals in the middle class. That might be a credible argument if IQ tests really measured

177

ability. What IQ tests measure is acquired information. Try the following IQ test and see how you do.

IQ TEST

1. What is <u>gray tape</u> and what is it used for?

2. What does <u>dissed</u> mean?

3. What are the <u>advantages</u> and <u>disadvantages</u> of moving often?

4. What is the <u>principal</u> kind of <u>work</u> that a <u>bondsman</u> does?

5. What is a <u>roach</u>?

6. How are a <u>pawnshop</u> and a <u>convenience store</u> alike? How are they different?

7. Why is it important for a non-US citizen to have a <u>green card</u>?

8. You go to the bakery store. You can buy five loaves of day old bread for 39 cents each or seven loaves of three day old bread for 28 cents each. Which choice will cost less?

9. What does **deportation** mean?

10. What is the difference between marriage and a common law relationship?

These questions are representative of the kinds of questions that are asked on IQ tests. This test is only different in one way - the content. Yet it illustrates clearly the point that the information tested on many IQ tests is only acquired knowledge. IQ tests were designed to predict success in school. However, they do not in any way predict ability or basic intelligence. If middle class students were to take this (invalidated) test, they could possibly have 9 IQ points fewer than many poor students. Therefore, the assessments and tests we use in many areas of school are not about ability or intelligence. They are about an acquired knowledge base; if your parents are educated, chances are that you will have a higher acquired knowledge base. A more honest approach to achievement is to look at teaching and learning.

179

2. DIFFERENTIATING BETWEEN TEACHING AND LEARNING

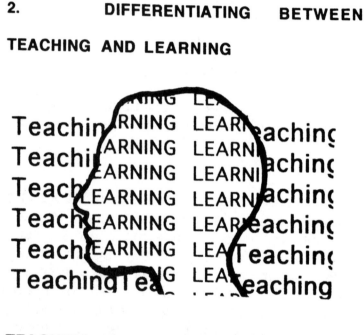

TEACHING IS WHAT OCCURS OUTSIDE OF THE HEAD.

LEARNING IS WHAT OCCURS INSIDE OF THE HEAD.

180

The emphasis during the last fifteen years in education has been on teaching. The theory has been that if you teach well enough, then learning will occur. But we all know of situations and individuals, including ourselves, who decided in a given situation not to learn. And we have all been in situations where we found it virtually impossible to learn because we did not have the background information or the belief system to accept it, even though it was well taught and presented.

In order to learn, an individual must have certain cognitive skills and must have a structure inside his/her head to accept the learning - a file cabinet or a piece of software. Traditionally, we have given the research on teaching to teachers and the research on learning to counselors and early childhood teachers. It is the research on learning that must be addressed if we are to work with students from poverty.

LEARNING STRUCTURES

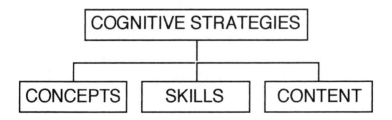

In this oversimplified representation of a learning structure are four things. The first is **cognitive strategies.** These are even more basic than concepts. They are fundamental ways of processing information. They are the infrastructure of the mind. **Concepts** store information and allow for retrieval. **Skills**, i.e. reading, writing, computing, language, are the processing of content. **Content** is the what of learning - the information used to make sense of daily life. Traditionally in schools we have assumed that the cognitive strategies are in place. If they are not, we test and place the student in a special program - special education, dyslexia, chapter 1, ADHD, 504, etc. No attempt is made to address the cognitive strategies because we believe they are to a large extent not remediable. We focus our efforts in Pre K and K on building concepts. We devote first through third grade to building skills. We enhance those skills in grades four and five. And when the student gets into sixth grade and onto the twelfth grade, we teach content.

The truth is that we can no longer pretend this arrangement works - no matter how well or how hard one teaches. Increasingly, students, mostly from poverty, are coming to school without the concepts, but more importantly, without the cognitive strategies. We simply cannot assign them all to special education. What are these cognitive strategies and how do we build learning structures inside the heads of students?

COGNITIVE STRATEGIES

Compelling work in this area has been done by a man named Reuven Feuerstein, an Israeli. He began in 1945 working with poor, disenfranchised Jewish youth who settled in Israel after World War II. He had studied under Piaget and disagreed with Piaget in one major way. He felt that between the environmental stimulus and the response should be mediation, i.e. the intervention of an adult.

	MEDIATION	
Identification of the **stimulus**	Assignment of **meaning**	Identification of **a strategy**

Mediation is basically three things - identification of the stimulus, assignment of meaning, and identification of a strategy. For example, we say to a child - "Don't cross the street. You could get hit by a car. So if you must cross the street, look both ways twice."

WHY IS MEDIATION SO IMPORTANT?

MEDIATION BUILDS COGNITIVE STRATEGIES AND THOSE STRATEGIES GIVE INDIVIDUALS THE ABILITY TO PLAN, SYSTEMATICALLY GO THROUGH DATA, ETC.

IF AN INDIVIDUAL DEPENDS UPON A RANDOM, EPISODIC STORY STRUCTURE FOR MEMORY PATTERNS, LIVES IN AN UNPREDICTABLE ENVIRONMENT, **AND HAS NOT DEVELOPED THE ABILITY TO PLAN**; THEN

IF AN INDIVIDUAL CANNOT PLAN, HE OR SHE **CANNOT PREDICT.**

IF AN INDIVIDUAL CANNOT PREDICT, HE OR SHE **CANNOT IDENTIFY CAUSE AND EFFECT.**

IF AN INDIVIDUAL CANNOT IDENTIFY CAUSE AND EFFECT, HE OR SHE **CANNOT IDENTIFY CONSEQUENCE.**

IF AN INDIVIDUAL CANNOT IDENTIFY CONSEQUENCE, HE OR SHE **CANNOT CONTROL IMPULSIVITY.**

IF AN INDIVIDUAL CANNOT CONTROL IMPULSIVITY, HE OR SHE **HAS AN INCLINATION TO CRIMINAL BEHAVIOR.**

184

Feuerstein identified the missing links that occurred in the mind when mediation had not occurred. These students by any standard would have been identified as special education students. Yet, with his program, many of these students who came to him in the mid-teens went on to be very successful, with some even completing Ph.D.'s. To teach these strategies, Feuerstein developed over 50 instruments.   What are these missing cognitive strategies?

MISSING   LINKS   (Feuerstein,   1980; Sharron, 1994)

1. "MEDIATED FOCUSING"- to focus attention and see objects in detail - opposite of blurred and sweeping perceptions.

2. "MEDIATED SCHEDULING"- based on routine. Ability to schedule and plan ahead. Ability to represent the future abstractly and therefore set goals.

3. "MEDIATION OF POSITIVE ANTICIPATION "- ability to control present for a happy representation of the future.

185

4. "MEDIATION OF INHIBITION AND CONTROL"-ability to defer gratification, think before acting, control impulsiveness

5. "MEDIATED REPRESENTATION OF THE FUTURE" - ability to construe imaginatively a future scenario based on facts.

6. "MEDIATION OF VERBAL STIMULATION"- use of precise language for defining and categorizing environment

7. "MEDIATED PRECISION"-ability to precisely define situations, things, people, etc. and use that precision for problem-solving.

MISSING LINKS/MEDIATIONS RESULT IN COGNITIVE DEFICIENCIES.

WHAT ARE THESE COGNITIVE DEFICIENCIES?

Blurred and sweeping perception and a lack of a systematic method of exploration means that these students have no consistent or predictable way of getting information. They see only about 50% of what is on a page. If you watch one of these students, in a new setting, they will rapidly go from object to object, touching everything - yet when you ask them what they have seen, they cannot tell you. This area is related to the use of the casual register story structure which is episodic and random in the details or information presented. They simply do not have cognitive methodology for doing tasks nor a systematic way to finish tasks.

Impaired verbal tools means that they do not have the vocabulary to deal with the cognitive tasks. Vocabulary words are the building blocks of the internal learning structure. Vocabulary is also the tool to better define a problem, seek more accurate solutions, etc. Many students who only rely on casual register do not use or have many prepositions or adverbs in their speech.

Impaired spatial orientation is simply the ability to orient objects, people, etc. in space. Directions, location, object size, object shape, etc. are not available to them. They do not have the vocabulary or the concepts for spatial orientation.

Impaired temporal orientation is the ability to organize and measure in time. One of Feuerstein's observations was that these students assign time to incidents on the basis of the emotional intensity of the experience, not the measured time that is a part of educated thinking. I find among students from poverty that time is not measured or heeded. Being somewhere on time is not valued. Time is not seen as a thing to be used or valued.

Impaired observations of constancies is the ability of the brain to hold an object inside the head and keep the memory of the object constant. In other words, when there is impaired observations of constancies, objects change shape and size in the brain. If this is the case, then learning alphabet letters, retaining shapes, etc. is problematic. It is also the ability to know what stays the same and what changes. For example, east and west are always constant; left and right change based on the orientation of the moment.

Lack of precision and accuracy in data gathering is another cognitive deficiency. It is related to several of the above deficiencies. Problem solving and other tasks are extremely problematic because they do not have the strategies to gather precise and accurate data.

Another cognitive deficiency is the ability to hold two objects or two sources inside the head while comparing and contrasting. If a student is unable to do this, he/she cannot assign information to categories inside his/her brain. If a student cannot assign information to categories, then he/she cannot retrieve the information except in an associative, random way.

These deficiencies explain many of the behaviors we see from students. How do we make interventions?

WHAT ARE THESE COGNITIVE STRATEGIES THAT MUST BE BUILT?

Feuerstein identified three stages in the learning process: " input, elaboration, and output."

INPUT STRATEGIES
Input is defined as the "quantity and quality of the data gathered."

1. **Use planning behaviors.**
2. **Focus perception on specific stimulus.**
3. **Control impulsivity.**
4. **Explore data systematically.**
5. **Use appropriate and accurate labels.**
6. **Organize space with stable systems of reference.**
7. **Orient data in time.**
8. **Identify constancies across variations.**
9. **Gather precise and accurate data.**

10. **Consider two sources of information at once.**
11. **Organize data (parts of a whole).**
12. **Visually transport data.**

ELABORATION STRATEGIES

Elaboration strategies are defined as the "use of the data."

1. **Identify and define the problem.**
2. **Select relevant cues.**
3. **Compare data.**
4. **Select appropriate categories of time.**
5. **Summarize data.**
6. **Project relationships of data.**
7. **Use logical data.**
8. **Test hypothesis.**
9. **Build inferences.**
10. **Make a plan using the data.**
11. **Use appropriate labels.**
12. **Use data systematically.**

OUTPUT STRATEGIES

Ouput is defined as the "communication of the data."

1. **Communicate clearly the labels and process.**
2. **Visually transports data correctly.**
3. **Uses precise and accurate language.**
4. **Controls impulsive behavior.**

What do these strategies mean?

Mediation builds these strategies. When these strategies are not present, they can be built. Typically in school, we begin teaching at the elaboration level, i.e. the use of the data. When students do not understand, we reteach these strategies but do not revisit the quality and quantity of the data gathered.

Input strategies (quantity and quality of data)

Planning behaviors include goal setting, identifying the procedures in the task, identifying the parts of the task, assigning time to the task(s), identifying the quality of the work necessary to complete the task.

Focus perception on specific stimulus is the strategy of seeing every detail on the page or in the environment. It is the strategy of identifying everything noticed by the five senses.

Control impulsivity is the strategy of stopping action until thinking about the task is done. There is a direct correlation with impulsivity control and improved behavior and achievement.

Explore data systematically means that a strategy is employed to procedurally and systematically go through every piece of data. Numbering is a way to go systematically through data. Highlighting each piece of data can be another method.

Use appropriate and accurate labels is the use of precise words and vocabulary to identify and explain. If a student does not have specific words to use, then his/her ability to retrieve and use information is severely limited. It is not enough that a student can do a task, he/she must also be able to label the procedures, tasks, and processes so that the task can be successfully repeated each time and analyzed at a metacognitive level. Metacognition is the ability to think about ones thinking. To do so, labels must be attached. Only when labels are attached can the task be evaluated and therefore, improved.

Organize space with stable systems of reference is crucial to success in math. It means that up, down, right, left, across, horizontal, vertical, diagonal, etc. are understood. It means that an individual can identify what the position of an item is with labels. It means that an individual can organize space. For

192

example, if an individual does not have this strategy, then it is virtually impossible to tell a p, b, and d apart. The only differentiation is the orientation in space.

Orient data in time is the strategy of assigning abstract values to time and the measurement of time. This strategy is crucial for identifying cause and effect, for determining sequence, and for predicting consequences.

Identify constancies across variations is the strategy of knowing what always remains the same and what changes. For example, if you do not know what always makes a square a square, you cannot identify constancies. It allows one to define things, to recognize a person or an object, and to compare and contrast. This strategy allows cursive writing to be read with all of its variations. I asked a group of fifth grade students I was working with this question: "If you saw me tomorrow, what about me would be the same and what would be different?" Many of the students had difficulty with that strategy.

Gather precise and accurate data is the strategy of using accurate labels, identifying the orientation in time and in space, knowing the constancies, and exploring the data systematically.

<u>Consider two sources of information</u> <u>at once</u> is the strategy of visually transporting data accurately, identifying the constancies and variations, and exploring the data systematically. When that is done, then precise and accurate labels need to be assigned.

<u>Organize data (parts of a whole)</u> involves exploring data systematically, organizing space, identifying constancies and variations, and labeling the parts and the whole with precise words.

<u>Visually transporting data</u> is when the eye picks up the data, carries it accurately to the brain, examines it for constancies and variations and labels the parts and whole.

Elaboration and output strategies tend to be fairly well understood in schools because that is where the teaching tends to occur.

194

WHAT WOULD LESSON DESIGN LOOK LIKE WHEN THESE STRATEGIES ARE TAUGHT?

The lesson would center around what the student would do. Sometime during the lesson, students would need to exhibit these five things:

The student would:	
	Use planning behaviors.
	Control impulsivity.
	Use evaluative behaviors.
	Explore data systematically.
	Use specific language.

Regardless of content, if the lesson required that in some way students did these five things, cognitive strategies would be strengthened, discipline would improve, and achievement would be enhanced.

TO TEACH A SPECIFIC STRATEGY OR STRATEGIES, THE FOLLOWING LESSON DESIGN COULD BE USED.

1. MAIN IDEA	People use rules to organize their world.
2. BRIDGING QUESTIONS	What are rules? What happens when there are no rules? Why do we need rules? Give me examples where we follow rules. Are there rules in nature? about driving? in sports?
3. STRATEGIES	a. focus perception on specific stimulus b. visually transport data c. explore data systematically. d. use specific language
4. LABELS	vertical, diagonally, model, relationship standard, frame, constant, lines, specific, shapes, size,
5. APPLICATION	What are the rules we are using today to do math? What are the rules about fractions?

This is a sample lesson that might be used in math to teach specific strategies. The reason that all five components need to be a part of the direct teaching of the strategy is that strategies and labels must be tied to concepts (main idea) so that the mind can retrieve, find, and use the information. To make that linkage occur, the bridging questions and application questions are crucial.

USING EYE MOVEMENT TO FOLLOW THE LEARNING AND PROCESSING

Bandler and Grinder (1979) did a great deal of work with non-verbal cues and cognitive processing. This work is known as neuro-linguistic programming. But of particular interest to educators is the work on eye movement because it allows a teacher to begin understanding the way(s) in which a student is processing information. Criminologists use these techniques to break crimes, lawyers use it to cross examine witnesses, and salespeople use it to enhance sales. Influencing with Integrity by Laborde (1983) is a lay persons' explanation of the information. Briefly, however, the main concepts will be explained.

Think of your face as a clock. It is as you look at the face. To begin, the face will have three zones: when the eyes are in the top zone, the individual is processing visual information. When eyes are in the middle zone, the individual is processing auditory information (with one exception). When

197

eyes are in the bottom zone, the individual is either talking to him/her self or processing feelings.

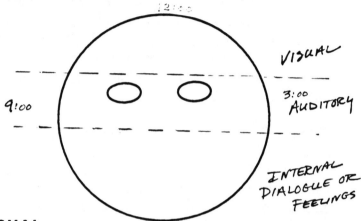

VISUAL

Now, let's go to the next level of information. If the person being observed has a tendency to be right handed, then the 2:00 o'clock position indicates that the individual is processing visually remembered data. Around 10:00 o'clock the individual is processing data that is visually constructed, in other words, the individual is putting together data from several sources. If the individual is left-handed, then 2:00 o'clock is visually constructed and 10:00 o'clock is visually remembered.

AUDITORY

If an individual is right-handed, 3:00 o'clock position indicates auditory remembered and 9:00 o'clock position indicates auditory constructed. If the individual is left-handed, then 3:00 is auditory constructed and 9:00 is auditory remembered.

FEELING/KINESTHETIC

If the individual is right-handed, the 5:00 o'clock position will be auditory internal dialogue and the 7:00 o'clock position will be feelings. If the individual is left-handed, then 5:00 o'clock is feelings and 7:00 o'clock is auditory internal dialogue.

VISUAL CONSTRUCT

If eyes are staring straight ahead and defocused, the individual is in a visual construct position.

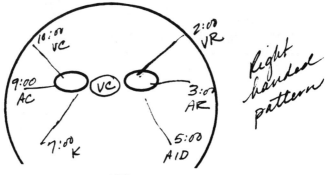

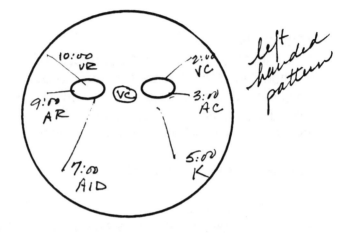

How does knowing eye movement help a teacher? If a student has moved his/her eyes to a visual position, then the teacher knows that the student is trying to find the information visually. The teacher can enhance the process by asking the student, "What do you see?" If the student is processing from an auditory position, the teacher can ask, "What do you remember hearing? " The other positions would be the same. It can help the teacher identify how a student tends to store and retrieve information.

ADDITIONAL INSTRUCTIONAL INTERVENTIONS WHICH BUILD CONCEPTUAL FRAMEWORKS AND COGNITVE STRATEGIES

* (For a comprehensive research-based overview, see Idol and Jones, 1991)

1. Using graphic organizers. (Idol and Jones, Chapter 3; 1991) Graphic organizers give students the ability to identify main concepts, assign specific labels to concepts, and sort relevant and non-relevent cues.

EXAMPLE:

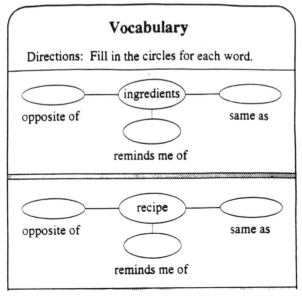

EXAMPLE:

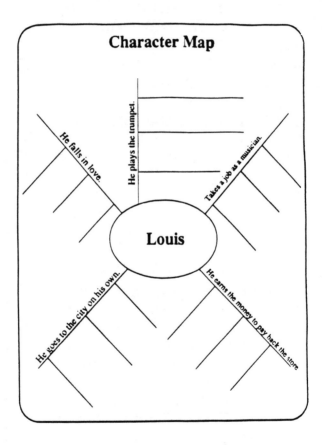

2. Identifying methods of having a systematic approach to the data/text. One way to do this is to provide students a systematic method to go through text. Some teachers had students highlight information. Here is one example:

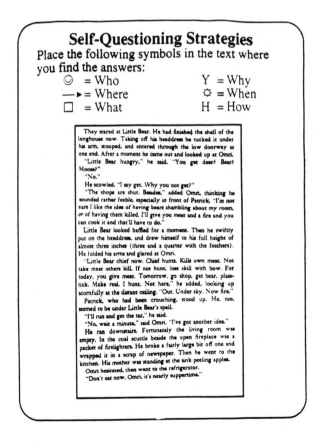

3. **Goal setting and procedural self-talk**
(Marzano and Arredondo, 1986) These two
activities should be a part of daily instruction. The
procedural self-talk can be written down and
eventually will become a part of the internal self-
talk. Goal setting addresses several cognitive
deficiencies.

**4. Teaching conceptual frameworks as part
of the content** (Marzano and Arredondo, 1986)
There are many ways to do this. One is by using
graphic organizers. Another is to teach content in
an associative way, i.e. teaching it in relationship to
what they personally have experienced rather than
in a linear or hierarchical way. Another way to
build conceptual frameworks is to take what they
know and translate it into the new form. For
example, having them write in casual register and
then translate into formal register. Or, having them
rewrite the story in a poverty structure. In other
words, it is the opportunity for students to see the
same information in more than one structure. In
math students would both draw the problem and do
the problem in an equation.

5. **Using a kinesthetic approach** as part of the
classroom environment is another intervention. For
example, rather than teaching algebra from strictly
equations on paper and pencil, the shop teacher
and the algebra teacher would design a project that

would require students to use algebra to design and complete a metalworking project. The Tech Prep program uses this approach.

6. **Use of rubrics** which show the levels of performance so that a student can begin to critique his/her expertise. What a well written rubric can do for a student is to allow him/her to evaluate his performance and how to improve on that performance. It allows the student to begin to address the cognitive deficiency of not being able to plan or schedule. It allows for the cognitive strategy of future representation to be developed because the student can see ahead of time the consequences of his/her choices.

7. **Teaching the structure of language.** Project Read is one such intervention and is a multi-sensory approach to teaching reading and writing. The focus is on teaching structure and patterns so that the student can understand the use of language in formal registers. The campuses in Goose Creek ISD which have implemented this program have significantly higher state test scores than those campuses that have not. (For more information about Project Read, contact Karen Coffey at 713/420-4408.)

8. **Teaching students to make questions** (Palincsar and Brown, 1984). There is a significant

relationship between the ability to ask a question syntactically and comprehension of text.

To teach students question making, simply give them this list of question stems and then use the text to make their own questions. Make them make four answer choices as well. Also, one can use the reciprocal teaching methods designed by Palincsar and Brown.

Question Making Stems

1. From this story/passage, how might _____ be described?

2. Why was _____?

3. Why did _____?

4. How else might the author have ended the story?

5. How might the story be different if _____?

6. (Use the word in a sentence from the story.) In this story, what does _____ mean?

7. What does the author of this article most probably believe?

8. How did _____ feel about_____?

9. What caused _____ to _____?

10. What is _____?

11. When _____ happened, why did _____?

12. The article/story states that _____. Why is that information important to the reader?

9. **Sorting relevant from irrelvent cues.**

Cartooning is a wonderful way to do this. Make students draw in six frames the main points of the text or story.

WHAT DOES THE RESEARCH SAY?

INSISTENCE

S UPPORT

EXPECTATIONS

If the research had to be summed up in three words, these are the three that seem to appear repeatedly. Traditionally in schools we have provided insistence and the last twenty years we have added expectations as a part of the discussion. It is the notion of support that must be provided to students now.

What is appropriate support? I am not talking about a munchy-fuzzy-feel-good notion of support. I am talking about what girders provide to a bridge. The supports these students need are cognitive strategies, appropriate relationships, coping strategies, goal setting opportunities, and appropriate instruction both in content and discipline. <u>The true discrimination that comes out of poverty is the lack of cognitive strategies. Those unseen attributes handicap the individual who does not have them in every aspect of life.</u>

The Virginia State Department of Education (1993) identified these four responses as being effective in promoting learning for at-risk students:

developmental preschool programs, supplemental reading programs, reducing class size, and schoolwide projects in prevention and support. These four responses could allow for relationships, support, insistence and development of cognitive strategies. A study of poor schools (in which some children achieve) looked at the external resources that students bring to the school. (Anderson, Hollinger, Conaty. 1993) What seems to be more important than involvement and coming to school by parents is whether parents provide support, insistence, and expectations at home. Perhaps we need to rethink the focus of parent training.

In conclusion, as we adapt and flex our instruction to meet the needs of these students, cognitive strategies and support need to be integrated with insistence and expectations.

WHAT DOES THIS INFORMATION MEAN IN THE SCHOOL OR WORK SETTING?

* The focus in schools should be on learning.

* Instruction in the cognitive strategies should be a part of the curriculum.

* Staff development should focus on a diagnostic approach rather than a programmatic approach.

* Efforts to promote learning should pay greater attention to what is in the student's head.

* Support, insistence, and expectations need to be guiding lights in our decisions about instruction.

210

CHAPTER NINE: CREATING RELATIONSHIPS

The key to achievement for students from poverty is in creating relationships with them. **No significant learning occurs without a**

significant relationship. Because poverty is about relationships as well as entertainment, the most significant motivator for these students is relationships.

The question becomes - How does a formal institution create relationships? Two sources provide some answers for this question. These sources are 1)the recent research in the field of science and 2) the work Covey has done with personal effectiveness.

Margaret Wheatley, in her book <u>Leadership and the New Science</u>, (1992) states quite clearly,

"Scientists in many different disciplines are questioning whether we can adequately explain how the world works by using the machine imagery created in the seventeenth century, most notably by Sir Issac Newton. In the machine model, one must understand parts. Things can be taken apart, dissected literally or representationally ....and then put back together without any significant loss. ....The Newtonian model of the world is characterized by materialism and reductionism - a focus on things rather than relationships.... The quantum view of reality strikes against most of our notions of reality. Even to scientists, it is admittedly bizarre. **But it is a world where *relationship* is the key determiner of what is observed**

and of how particles manifest themselves.....Many scientists now work with the concept of fields - invisible forces that structure space or behavior." (p 8-13)

Wheatley goes on to say that in the new science of quantum physics physical reality is not just tangible, it is also intangible. Fields are invisible yet they are the "substance of the universe....In organizations, which is the more important influence on behavior - the system or the individual? The quantum world answered that question....It depends. ...**What is critical is the relationship created between the person and the setting**. That relationship will always be different, will always evoke different potentialities. *It all depends on the players and the moment.*" (34-35)

Teachers and administrators have always known that the relationships, often referred to as "politics" made a great deal of difference,-- sometimes all of the differences,-- in what could or could not happen in a building. Yet for the last fifteen years, we have concentrated all our research in schools on "achievement" and "effective teaching strategies." We used the Newtonian approach to teaching, dissecting it into parts. Yet, the most important part of learning seems to be related to relationship, if we listen to the data and the potent realities indicated in the

213

research emerging from the disciplines of biology and physics.

When students who have been in poverty and have successfully made it into middle class are asked how they made the journey, the answer nine times out of ten has to do with a relationship - a teacher, counselor, or coach who made a suggestion or took an interest in them as individuals.

Covey (1989) uses the notion of an emotional bank account to relay the crucial aspects of relationships. He indicates that in all relationships one makes deposits to and withdrawals from the other individual in that relationship. In his words, the following are the deposits and withdrawals.

DEPOSITS	WITHDRAWALS
Seek first to understand	Seek first to be understood
Keeping promises	Breaking promises
Kindnesses, Courtesies	Unkindnesses, discourtesies
Clarifying expectations	Violating expectations
Loyalty to the absent	Disloyalty, duplicity
Apologies	Pride, conceit, arrogance
Open to feedback	Rejecting feedback

This chart taken from <u>The Seven Habits of Highly Effective People</u>.

The first step to creating relationships with students and adults is to make the deposits that are the basis of relationships. Relationships always begin as one individual to another. First and foremost in all relationships with students, is the relationship between each teacher and student, between each student and administrator, and then, among all of the players, including student to student relationships.

What then is meant by relationship? (Should students become my personal friends? Should I go out with them?) A successful relationship occurs when emotional deposits are made to the student, emotional withdrawals are avoided, and students are respected. Are there boundaries to the relationship? Absolutely - and that is what is meant by clarifying expectations. But to honor students as human beings is to establish a relationship that will provide for enhanced learning.

What are the deposits and withdrawals made to students from poverty?

DEPOSIT TO INDIVIDUAL FROM POVERTY	WITHDRAWAL MADE FROM INDIVIDUAL IN POVERTY
Appreciation for humor and entertainment provided by the individual	Put downs or sarcasm about the humor or the individual
Acceptance of what the individual cannot say about a person or situation	Insistence and demands for full explanation about a person or situation
Respect for the demands and priorities of relationships	Insistence on the middle class view of relationships.
Using the adult voice	Using the parent voice.
Assisting with goal setting.	Telling the individual his/her goals.
Identifying options related to available resources	Making judgments on the value and availability of resources
Understanding the importance of personal freedom, speech, and individual personality	Assigning pejorative character traits to the individual

By understanding deposits that are valued by

poor students, the relationship is stronger.

216

How does an organization or school begin to create relationships? Through support systems, through caring about students, by promoting student achievement, by being role models, by insisting upon successful behaviors for school. **Support systems are simply networks of relationships**.

Will creating healthy relationships with students make all students successful? No. But if we make a difference for 5% more of our students the first year and 5% more each year thereafter, we will have progressed considerably from where we are right now.

In the final analysis, as one looks back on his or her teaching career, it is the relationships one remembers.

WHAT DOES THIS INFORMATION MEAN IN THE SCHOOL OR WORK SETTING?

* For students from poverty, the motivation for their success will be in the relationships.

✓ CONCLUSION

One of the topics as yet untouched is the need to grieve and go through the grieving process as one teaches or works with the poor. The stages in the grieving process include anger, denial, bargaining, depression and acceptance. As one meets and works with a particular family or individual, there is such frustration and ultimately, grieving, because many situations are so embedded as to be hopeless. It is like dealing with the legendary octopus, each time a tenacle is removed, another appears. Particularly for the adults, so many choices have been made that virtually preclude any resolution that would be acceptable from an educated perspective. Yet, the role of the educator or social worker or employer is not to save the individual, but rather to offer a support system, role models, and opportunities to learn which will increase the likelihood of the individual's success. Ultimately, the choice always belongs to the individual.

Yet another notion among the middle class and educated is that if the poor had a choice, they would live differently. The financial resources would certainly help make a difference. Even with the financial resources, not each individual who received those finances would choose to live differently. There is a freedom of verbal expression, an appreciation of individual personality, a heightened and intense emotional experience, and a sensual, kinesthetic approach to life that is not available in the middle class or among the educated. Those are so embedded into the daily life of the poor that to have those cut off would be to loose a limb. Many choose not to live a different life. And for some, alcoholism, laziness, lack of motivation, drug addiction, etc. make the choices for the individual.

But it is the responsibility of educators and others who work with the poor to teach the differences and skills/rules that will allow the individual to make the choice. As it stands now, for many of the poor, the choice never exists.

✓ STATISTICAL CHARTS ON POVERTY

These three charts are taken from the United States census data and were provided to Texas educators as part of the Texas School Improvement Initiative training in 1995. This training is sponsored through the Texas Education Agency, Austin, Texas.

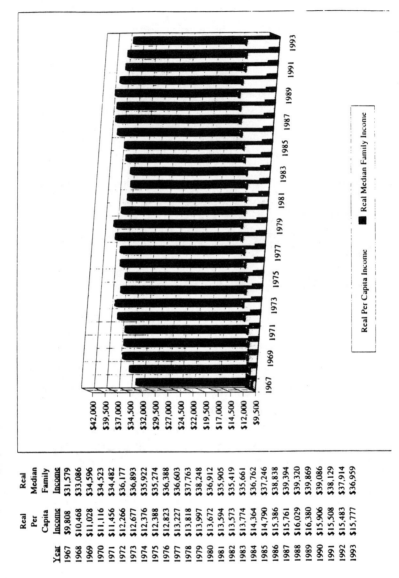

U.S. PER CAPITA AND MEDIAN FAMILY INCOME, IN 1993 DOLLARS: 1967 TO 1993

Year	Real Per Capita Income	Real Median Family Income
1967	$9,808	$31,579
1968	$10,468	$33,086
1969	$11,028	$34,596
1970	$11,116	$34,523
1971	$11,456	$34,482
1972	$12,266	$36,177
1973	$12,677	$36,893
1974	$12,376	$35,922
1975	$12,388	$35,274
1976	$12,823	$36,388
1977	$13,227	$36,603
1978	$13,818	$37,763
1979	$13,997	$38,248
1980	$13,672	$36,912
1981	$13,594	$35,905
1982	$13,573	$35,419
1983	$13,774	$35,661
1984	$14,364	$36,762
1985	$14,790	$37,246
1986	$15,386	$38,838
1987	$15,761	$39,394
1988	$16,029	$39,320
1989	$16,380	$39,869
1990	$15,906	$39,086
1991	$15,508	$38,129
1992	$15,483	$37,914
1993	$15,777	$36,959

SOURCE: U.S. Bureau of the Census.

222

U.S. MEDIAN INCOME FOR PERSONS AGE 25 AND OLDER, BY SEX AND EDUCATIONAL ATTAINMENT: 1993

Sex	Overall	Grade Less Than 9th grade	Grade 9-12 (no diploma)	HS graduate (includes GED)	Associate Degree	Bachelors Degree	Masters Degree	Profes-sional Degree	Doctorate Degree
				Number of Persons with Income (in thousands)					
Male	76,419	6,734	7,377	24,682	4,901	12,360	4,320	1,650	1,149
Female	80,898	6,423	8,152	29,171	6,282	11,447	4,003	583	447
				Median Income, in Current Dollars					
Male	$24,605	$10,895	$14,550	$21,782	$29,736	$37,474	$45,597	$69,678	$55,751
Female	$12,234	$6,480	$7,187	$11,089	$18,346	$22,452	$31,389	$32,742	$42,737

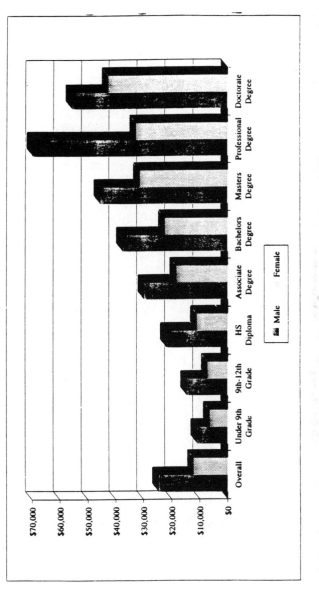

PERCENT OF U.S. PERSONS BELOW POVERTY LEVEL, BY RACE AND ETHNICITY: 1976 TO 1993

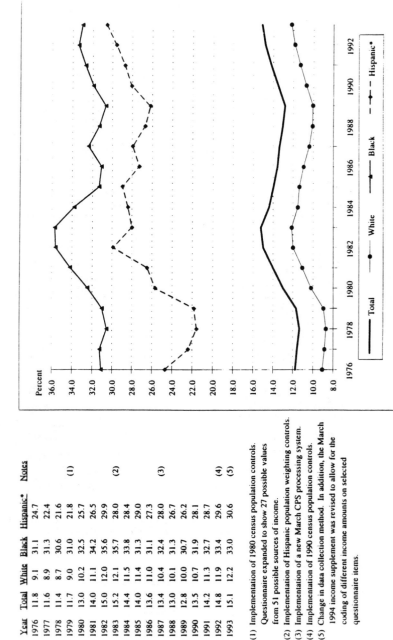

Year	Total	White	Black	Hispanic*	Notes
1976	11.8	9.1	31.1	24.7	
1977	11.6	8.9	31.3	22.4	
1978	11.4	8.7	30.6	21.6	
1979	11.7	9.0	31.0	21.8	(1)
1980	13.0	10.2	32.5	25.7	
1981	14.0	11.1	34.2	26.5	
1982	15.0	12.0	35.6	29.9	
1983	15.2	12.1	35.7	28.0	(2)
1984	14.4	11.5	33.8	28.4	
1985	14.0	11.4	31.3	29.0	
1986	13.6	11.0	31.1	27.3	
1987	13.4	10.4	32.4	28.0	(3)
1988	13.0	10.1	31.3	26.7	
1989	12.8	10.0	30.7	26.2	
1990	13.5	10.7	31.9	28.1	
1991	14.2	11.3	32.7	28.7	
1992	14.8	11.9	33.4	29.6	(4)
1993	15.1	12.2	33.0	30.6	(5)

(1) Implementation of 1980 census population controls.
    Questionnaire expanded to show 27 possible values
    from 51 possible sources of income.

(2) Implementation of Hispanic population weighting controls.

(3) Implementation of a new March CPS processing system.

(4) Implementation of 1990 census population controls.

(5) Change in data collection method. In addition, the March
    1994 income supplement was revised to allow for the
    coding of different income amounts on selected
    questionnaire items.

224

* Hispanics can be of any race.

SOURCE: U.S. Bureau of the Census.

✔BIBLIOGRAPHY

Anderson, Judith; Hollinger, Debra; and Conaty, Joseph. (1993). Re-examining the Relationship Between School Poverty and Student Achievement. *ERS Spectrum.* Spring. p 21-31.

Bandler, Richard and John Grinder. (1979) *Frogs into Princes.* Moab, UT: Real People Press.

Barnitz, John G. (1994). Discourse Diversity: Principles for Authentic Talk and Literacy Instruction. *Classroom Talk about Text: What Teenagers and Teachers come to Know about the World through Talk about Text.* Rosalind Horowitz, Ed. International Reading Association publication.

Bianchi, Suzanne M. (1990). America's Children: Mixed Prospects. *Population Bulletin.* Volume 45. Number 1. June.

Boals, Beverly, M. et al. (1990) *Children in Poverty:Providing and Promoting a Quality Education.* ERIC Document.

Bradshaw, John. (1988). *Bradshaw on : The Family.* Health Communications: Deerfield Beach, Florida.

Connell, R.W. (1994). *Poverty and Education.* Harvard Educational Review. Vol.64. No. 2. Summer.

Coontz, Stephanie. (1995). The American Family and the Nostalgia Trap. *Phi Delta Kappan.* Volume 76. Number 7. March.

Cook, John T. and Brown, Larry J. (1993). *Two Americas: Racial Differences in Child Poverty in the U.S. A Linear Trend Analysis to the Year 2010.* Research in Porgress Working Paper. Tufts University, Medord, Ma.

Covey, Stephen R. (1989). *The Seven Habits of Highly Effective People: Powerful Lessons in Personal Change.* New York: Simon and Schuster.

Edelman, Peter B.Ed and Ladner, Joyce, Ed. (1991). *Adolescence and Poverty: Challenge for the 1990's.* Center for National Policy. Washington, D.C.

Educational Attainments of Students Living in Poverty. Report of the Department of Education to the Governor and the General Assembly of Virginia. Senate Document No. 13. (1993). Virginia State Department of Education. Richmond, Va.

Einbinder, Susan D. (1993). *Five Million Children: 1993 Update.* Columbia University. New York, New York. National Center for Children in Poverty.

Eitzen, Stanley D. (1992). Problem Students: The Sociocultural Roots. *Phi Delta Kappan.* p 584-590. April.

Feuerstein, Reuven, et al. (1980). *Instrumental Enrichment: An Intervention Program for Cognitive Modifiability.* Scott, Foresman and Co. Glenview, IL.

Five Million Children: 1992 Update. (1992). Columbia University. New York, New York. National Center for Children in Poverty.

Gardner, Howard. (1991). *The Unschooled Mind: How Children Think and How Schools Should Teach.* Basic Books. New York, New York.

Garmezy, Norman. (1991). Resiliency and Vulnerability to Adverse Developmental Outcomes Associated with Poverty. *American Behavioral Scientist.* Volume 34. No. 4. p 416-30. March -April.

Gee, James Paul. (1987). What is Literacy? *Teaching and Learning: The Journal of Natural Inquiry.* Volume 2. Number 1. Fall.

Goleman, Daniel. (1995). *Emotional Intelligence.* Bantam Books, New York, New York.

Haberman, Martin. (1995). *Star Teachers of Children in Poverty.* Kappa Delta Pi. Madison, Wisconsin.

Harris, Lorwen Connie. (1988). Facts about Texas Children. Excerpted from *Children, Choice, and Change*. Hogg Foundation for Mental Health. Texas University. Austin, Texas.

Hodgkinson, Harold, L. (1995) What Should We Call People? Race, Class, and the Census for 2000. *Phi Delta Kappan*. October. 173-179.

Idol, Lorna and Jones, B.F., ed. (1991). *Educational Values and Cognitive Instruction: Implications for Reform*. Lawrence Erlbaum Associates. Hillsdale, New Jersey.

Jones, B. F., Pierce, J., and Hunter, B. (1988) Teaching students to construct graphic representations. *Educational Leadership*. 46 (4), 20-25.

Joos, Martin. (1967). The Styles of the Five Clocks. *Language and Cultural Diversity in American Education*. 1972. Abrahams, R.D. and Troike, R. C., Eds. Englewood Clifs, N.J. Prentice-Hall, Inc.

Marzano, Robert J. and Arredondo, Daisy. (1986). *Tactics for Thinking*. MCREL. Aurora, Co.

Montano-Harmon, Maria Rosario. (1991). Discourse Features of Written Mexican Spanish: Current Research in Contrastive Rhetoric and Its Implications. *Hispania*. Volume 74, Number 2, May 417-425.

Kaplan, R. B. (1984). Cultural Thought Patterns in Intercultural Education. In McKay, S., Ed. 1984. *Composing in a Second Language.* Rowley, MA. Newbury House Publishers, Inc. p 43-62

Knapp, Michael, s. etal. (1993). *Academic Challenge for the Children of Poverty. Study of Academic Instruction for Disadvantaged Students. Volume 1: Findings and Conclusions.* Policy Studies Associates, Inc. Washington, D.C.

Knapp, Michael S. and Shields, Patrick M., Eds. (1991). *Better Schooling for the Children of Poverty: Alternatives to Conventional Wisdom.* McCutchan Publishing Corporation. Berkeley, CA.

Knapp, Michael S. and Shields, Patrick M. (1990). *Reconceiving Academic Instruction for the Children of Poverty.* Phi Delta Kappan. June. p 753-758.

Laborde, Genie Z. (1983). *Influencing with Integrity: Management Skills for Communication and Negiotiation.* Syntony Publishing, Palo Alto, CA.

Language Barriers are More Complex than We Might Think. (1992). *CSBA News.* Sacramento, CA: California School Boards Association, Volume 4, No. 9. November.

Larson, Jackie. (1993). Maria Montano-Harmon: A Call for Heightened Awareness.*Texas Lone Star.* November.

Lewit, Eugene, M. (1993). Child Indicators: Children in Poverty. *Future-of-Children.* Volume 3. Number 1. p 176-82. Spring.

Lewit, Eugene, M. (1993). Why is Poverty Increasing Among Children? *Future-of-Children.* Volume 3. Number 2. Summer/Fall.

Making Schools Work for Children in Poverty: A New Framework Prepared by the Commission on Chapter 1. (1992). AASA, Washington, D.C. December.

Miranda, Leticia, C. (1991). *Latino Child Poverty in the United States.* Children's Defense Fund. Washington, D.C.

Moynihan, Daniel Patrick. (1989). Welfare Reform: Serving America's Children. *Teachers College Record.* Volume 90. Number 3. Spring.

Natale, Jo Anna. (1992) Growing Up the Hard Way. *American School Board Journal.* October. p 20-27.

Natriello, Gary; McGill, Edward, L. and Pallas, Aaron M. (1990). *Schooling Disadvantaged Children: Racing Against Catastrophe.* Teachers College Press. Columbia University, New York.

O'Neill, John. (1991). A Generation Adrift? *Educational Leadership.* September. p 4-10.

Palincsar, A. S., and Brown, A.L. (1984). The Reciprocal teaching of comprehension-fostering and comprehension-monitoring activities.

Cognition and Instruction. 1 (2), 117-175.

Renchler, Ron. (1993). Poverty and Learning. *ERIC Digest.* Number 83. Eric Clearinghouse on Educational Management, Eugene, Oregon.

Rural Children: Increasing Poverty Rates Pose Educational Challenges. Briefing Report to the Chairwoman, Congressional Rural Caucus, House of Representatives. (1994). General Accounting Office. Washington, D.C.

School Age Demographics: Recent Trends Pose New Educational Challenges. Briefing Report to Congressional Requesters. (1993). General Accounting Office. Washington, D.C.

Sharron, Howard and Coulter, Martha. (1994). *Changing Children's Minds: Feuerstein's Revolution in the Teaching of Intelligence.* BPC Wheatons Ltd., Exeter, Great Britain.

Stern, Mark J. (1987). The Welfare of Families. *Educational Leadership.* March. p 82-87.

Takeuchi, David, T. et al. (1991). Economic Stress in the Family and Children's Emotional and Behavioral Problems. *Journal of Marriage and the Family.* volume 53. Number 4. p 1031-41. November.

Texas School Improvement Initiative: Peer Evaluator Training Manual. (1995) Texas Education Agency. Austin, Texas.

231

Thornburg, Kathy R; Hoffman, Stevie; Remeika, Corinne. (1991). Youth at Risk: Society at Risk. *Elementary School Journal.* Volume 91. Number 3. p 199-208. January.

Vobejda, Barbara. (1994). Half of Nation's Kids Not in "Typical" Family. *Houston Chronicle.* Tuesday, August 30.

Wheatley, Margaret J. (1992). *Leadership and the New Science.* Berrett-Koehler Publishers. San Francisco, CA.

Woodard, Samuel L. (1992). Academic Excellence in the Urban Environment: Overcoming the Odds. *NASSP Bulletin.* Volume 76. Number 546. p 57-61. October.

Zill, Nicholaus. (1993). The Changing Realities of Family Life. *Aspen Institute Quarterly.* Volume 5. Number 1. p 27-51. Winter.

ABOUT THE AUTHOR

Ruby K. Payne has been a professional educator for twenty-four years. She has been a secondary teacher and department chairperson, an elementary principal, a consultant, and a central office administrator. She is now consulting and writing. She has given hundreds of workshops and has worked with several thousand teachers and administrators.

She has a B.A. from Goshen College, Goshen Indiana; a M.A. from Western Michigan University, Kalamazoo, Michigan; and a Ph.D. from Loyola University in Chicago.

She and her husband, Frank, have been married for twenty-three years and they have a son, Tom, who is thirteen.

RFT PUBLISHING CO
3411 GARTH ROAD, SUITE 229
BAYTOWN, TX 77521
1 800 424 9484
FAX: 281 420 7063

WANT YOUR OWN COPIES? WANT TO GIVE A COPY TO A
FRIEND?   PLEASE SEND ME:
_____ COPY OF <u>A FRAMEWORK: UNDERSTANDING</u>
<u>AND WORKING WITH STUDENTS AND ADULTS FROM</u>
<u>POVERTY</u> @ 22.00 by mail WORKSHOP PRICE: $15.00
MAIL ORDERS OF FIVE BOOKS OR MORE - $15.00 each

MAIL TO:

NAME   ORGANIZATION:

_____   _____

ADDRESS   CITY/STATE/ZIP

_____   _____

PHONE NUMBER

_____   _____

PAYMENT
                                                    SUBTOTAL_____
P.O. #
_____   SHIPPING: $2.00/book_____
SIGNATURE   7.25% sales tax in Texas_____

_____
CHECK ENCLOSED _____   TOTAL ENCLOSED_____